P9-DNK-935

Sacred Reading

The Ancient Art of *Lectio Divina*

Michael Casey

LIGUORI/TRIUMPH
Liguori, Missouri

Published by Liguori/Triumph
An Imprint of Liguori Publications
Liguori, Missouri

This edition published 1996 by special arrangement with HarperCollins*Religious*, a member of the HarperCollins*Publishers* (Australia) Pty Ltd group.

Library of Congress Cataloging-in-Publication Data

Casey, Michael, monk of Tarrawarra.
Sacred reading : the ancient art of lectio divina / Michael Casey.
p. cm.
Includes bibliographical references.
ISBN 0-89243-891-6
1. Bible—Reading. 2. Bible—Devotional use. 3. Spiritual life—Catholic Church. 4. Benedictines—Spiritual life. 5. Catholic Church—Doctrines. I. Title.
BS617.C27 1996
248.3—dc20 95–44569

All rights reserved. No part of this publication may be reproduced, stored in a retrieval system, or transmitted in any form or by any means—electronic, mechanical, photocopy, recording, or any other—except for brief quotations in printed reviews, without the prior permission of the publisher.

Copyright 1995 by Michael Casey
Printed in the United States of America
First U.S. Edition 1996
01 00 99 98 97 6 5 4 3

FOL2—

CONTENTS

For Brother Kevin Burke
A delightful example of the effects
of a lifetime's reading

On 17 April 1995,
after accepting this dedication,
in the 80th year of his life
and the 60th year of his
monastic profession,
Brother Kevin returned to God

In memoriam

PREFACE

In the wake of the Second Vatican Council much energy was expended by Catholic religious orders in trying to identify their distinctive gifts. It was hoped that this clearer vision would be not only a means of increasing their own sense of identity, but also a pointer toward the special service that each order had to offer to the Church. The Council insisted that the charisms of different ecclesial groups are intended for their own domestic enhancement, as well as for a wider diffusion. What is given to individuals and communities is intended ultimately for the enrichment of the whole of God's people.

All religious orders had to ask themselves the question: "What do we have to offer the people of God?" In many cases the answer concerned the different services provided by members of religious congregations and the spirit in which these services were rendered. With monastic communities the question was a little more difficult. Their gift consisted in the lessons learned from a very distinctive lifestyle – or rather, not the lifestyle itself, but the traditional wisdom contained in it that could be applied to different situations.

The monastic orders of the West mostly follow the Rule of Saint Benedict. This means that the after-shocks of Vatican II were absorbed more readily in the context of a fifteen hundred year history. Less was invested in the particularities of the immediate past. So much of pre-conciliar Catholicism was marked by the attitudes and devotions typical of the Counter-Reformation. Monastic spirituality predated this. With such a strong root system it was less traumatic to undertake the radical pruning of surface growth that the Council demanded. Part of what these older orders have to offer the Church of today derives from their antiquity. They serve as reminders that there is more to the Church than the habits and mind-sets of the past couple of centuries. In the work of renewal we have discovered that there are depths of human and Christian experience yet to be explored. The upheavals of recent decades will have had a good effect if they have caused the uncovering of hidden resources that can facilitate our creative interaction with contemporary realities.

Although practical difficulties abounded, at the level of theory the Council brought much confirmation to the "benedictine" tradition.[1] Many key elements of Vatican II were familiar to monks and nuns: the ecclesial vision, the emphasis on community over individualism, the renewed appreciation of liturgy and Scripture, the spirit of *humanitas*, the strong Christocentrism. These values had long been cherished in Western monasticism – even when they found less favor in the wider Church. They were enshrined, for instance, in the writings of Abbot Marmion, whose books were bread-and-butter reading not only for monastics but also for thousands of priests and religious – even bishops. In fact, it is probable that the majority of the Council Fathers had read Marmion at some stage in their career.[2] He may have exerted a hidden influence on the outcome of this providential gathering.

As the dust settled after the intensive house-cleaning initiated by the Council, monks and nuns began to appreciate more the spiritual heritage they had received in the monastic tradition. Increasingly through hospitality, writing, and speaking, they offered to the people of God the deep experiential wisdom of monastic tradition. For many, monastic spirituality came as a breath of fresh air. More people than ever before rejoice in their contact with monasteries and look to monastic spirituality to provide the unique blend of sobriety and affectivity that alone makes religion seem real. No matter that their daily lives are far removed from cloistral existence. The spirit of monasticism is broad and non-specific; it adapts readily to many different situations. This is probably why it has survived relatively intact over the centuries.

Primary among the elements of a monastic approach to God was the rediscovery of *lectio divina*,[3] the art of sacred reading. This is so different from the sort of reading we do to obtain information that some re-education is essential. *Lectio divina* is more than the pious perusal of "spiritual books." *Lectio divina* is a technique of prayer and a guide to living. It is a means of descending to the level of the heart and of finding God. In the past two decades many people have been initiated into *lectio*, although often this has been merely a matter of refining an existing practice. It has been a common experience to discover that binding prayer to the Scriptures is an effective means of overcoming the obstacle of subjectivism and of finding a way out of what had become a blind alley of blank spiritual experience.

During the 1970s many articles on *lectio divina* appeared. The term and the practice became reasonably familiar among those who frequent journals and books that deal with spirituality. What is significant is that a generation later there exists no book-length, "postgraduate" treatment of *lectio* from within the monastic tradition, suitable for those who have developed through its exercise over two decades.[4] This present book attempts to remedy this situation by reflecting on aspects of *lectio divina* that become important only after sustained practice. This necessarily involves some returning to fundamentals, but the focus of the book is on later developments. In particular this involves seeing *lectio* not only as a technique of prayer, but also as a preparation for contemplation. As a consequence there is a certain amount of overlap and ambiguity; much of what is said about reading applies equally to prayer and contemplation, and vice versa.

I think it also needs to be said that *Sacred Reading* is not itself intended as *lectio divina*. It is simply a book of instruction proposed for your critical reflection. Its ambition is to offer in accessible and somewhat systematic form a detailed exposition of a valuable traditional art. If readers can find something in it that will help them to take the next step of their journey toward God, the purpose of the book may be considered fulfilled.

To find answers to some of the questions that this inquiry raises, I have returned to tradition. To some degree *lectio divina* must be defined historically; it is the manner of reading ecclesial texts developed and practiced in benedictine monasteries. We can learn from the experience of ancient monks and nuns, even though our resultant practice does not exactly mirror theirs. At least it enables us to transcend some of our cultural blind spots, so that we perceive more fully the clarity of the revealed message. As it happens, we will probably find that some ancient emphases coincide with contemporary concerns. Some fusion of the horizons of past and present not only enables us to use centuries-old experience as a resource, but helps us to appreciate more the specific contributions of our own generation.

You will find in this book many references to Saint Benedict's Rule for monasteries and to other classical works of the monastic tradition. Western monastic practice is the matrix in which the art of sacred reading was formed. This is not to say that its practice is restricted to people in monasteries. My ambition is to describe *lectio divina* in such detail that those living outside monasteries and not in direct contact with the lived experience of monks and nuns can profit from their tradition in the living of the Gospel.

This is a book that intends to take the past seriously. My main concern, however, is with the present. If I seek answers from ancient wisdom it is only because my own experience and that of my contemporaries has raised questions that indicate a need to transcend the barriers of time and culture and to search more broadly. It is to embrace the past as a resource toward more effective living in the present. I am not advocating a return to the ways of antiquity. I am simply asserting that there are elements of universal human experience that are overlooked in our culture that can be rediscovered by paying attention to the insights of another time and situation. Nor am I proposing *lectio divina* as the only approach to prayer and life. I hope that most people who read this book will take from it what they need and reach their own synthesis. Tradition is meant to be a servant of the present and the future, not a tyrant imposing its own preferences on a very different world.

Those who have read by book *Toward God: The Ancient Wisdom of Western Prayer* (Liguori/Triumph, Liguori, MO, 1996) will recognize some overlap between it and the present work. The two books share a single basic philosophy, although this book expands considerably the discussion of *lectio divina* begun in the seventh and eighth chapters of *Toward God.*

1

THE SPIRIT OF MONASTIC *LECTIO*

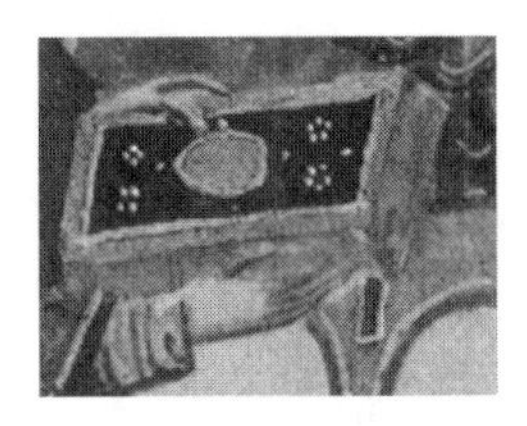

When Saint Benedict compiled his *Rule* for monasteries in the first part of the sixth century, he made provision for each monk to spend several hours every day reading or listening to books being read. This may not strike us as particularly extraordinary – given that monastic existence is generally considered fairly remote from ordinary living and monks often seem to be bookish people. In fact, there are several oddities about Saint Benedict's recommendation that are worth considering since they demonstrate how crucial this practice was considered in leading a Christian life.

First of all, we need to note that the practice of personal reading was relatively unusual at this time. Books were scarce and reading skills were confined to those who had received a liberal education – a possibility rendered increasingly remote by the cataclysmic decline of the Roman Empire and the civilization it promoted. The availability of reading matter was not to be taken for granted. The process of copying an existing manuscript was long and required much diligence. From the preparation of parchment and ink to the copying of every word of text, the production of books required time and resources. In monetary terms, the cost of a book in modern reckoning would probably amount to thousands of dollars. The monks of the benedictine tradition regarded reading as an essential element in living a spiritual life and were prepared to invest considerable resources in ensuring that it would be possible both for themselves and for future generations.

It was the rarity of books that dictated the style of reading. Because the acquisition of a manuscript represented a considerable investment, only those books were copied that were considered to be of special value.[1] There was no place for light reading. As a result, whatever was read was approached with the expectation that it would be worthwhile. The critical instinct was held in check. The reader opened the book to be instructed by others wiser and more learned than himself. There was always respect for the text; in the case of the Bible and the works of the great Christian teachers this grew into a deep sense of reverence. The books themselves were common property and the choice of titles reflected the community's concerns. Even though the individual monk might read his own book and think his own thoughts, his reading tended to communion rather than alienation. Although there was room for individual variations, in general the solitary reader moved in the same universe of meaning as the rest of the community. Reading cemented existing relationships; it did not foment isolation. This was reinforced by the fact that monks usually read in common. Typically they sat around the cloister in silence, each absorbed by the volume before him. Books themselves were often cumbersome; they were not convenient for speed reading so the monks tended to read slowly, probably vocalizing the words as they read. Often significant passages would be committed to memory; only a few scholars had the possibility of taking notes for permanent reference. With so few titles available, favorite works would be re-read many times. Because there were few reference books or commentaries, the monks had to learn to sit with difficulties and obscurities and try to puzzle out for themselves the meaning of the page before them. Reading became a dialogue with the text. For most of the monks this sacred reading – either in the cloister or in the liturgy – was the only reading they did.

Many of us today who attempt to master the technique of *lectio divina* find that it becomes confused with other types of reading undertaken professionally or for entertainment or knowledge.[2] The specificity of the exercise can be difficult to maintain. This means that we have to make the effort to build into our holy reading some of the qualities that the ancient monks were lucky enough to have by accident. We have to theorize about reading more than they did. Ultimately, however, this will be to our advantage, since nothing is so practical as good theory.

Integrity of text

The longest section dealing with *lectio divina* in the Rule of Benedict occurs in the context of Lent.[3] For Benedict this is a season of personal and community renewal during which we water down our vices and try to become more attentive to the summons of grace. An essential component in this dynamic process is an increased amount of time allocated to holy reading. Benedict envisaged his monks making about three hours a day available for personal *lectio*. He sees reading as one of the sources of spiritual energy, something that puts us into contact with grace and thus makes possible an enhanced level of fervor and unselfishness in daily living.

It is clear that what Benedict has in mind is a very existential, life-related reading and not just mindless paging through any volume that comes to hand. He emphasizes this by giving a certain solemnity to the choice of a Lenten book and then instructing his monks that once selected the books are to be read through from beginning to end in their entirety: *Per ordinem ex integro*. This reflects a principle that Benedict advocates elsewhere in the Rule. Spend as much time as you need before making up your mind, but once you make a commitment, stay with it.

It is on this emphasis on the integrity of what we read that I wish to concentrate. This stability in the material read is one of the distinguishing marks of monastic *lectio divina*. This constancy is a matter of respect for the literary unity of what has been written. It does not mean that we have to read the Bible from beginning to end, spending forty years wandering in the desert of Leviticus. It is more a matter of reading whole books, if we are reading the Scriptures, and not just selections. If there is a question of using other texts, the same value needs to be observed, but how it is implemented will depend on the literary character of what we are reading.

One reason for this insistence is to avoid the danger of misinterpretation inherent in random reading. In most writings there is an internal dynamic. The author does not always come to the point immediately. Saint Paul, for example, does not begin by voicing his most pressing concerns, but first woos his readers to make them more receptive, prepares the ground by signalling his competence to speak, and lays theological foundations. Only then does the real import of the writing reveal itself. The whole epistle is a unity; one part cannot be understood sensibly without reference to the totality. The practical suggestions at the end may be easy enough to follow, but without the preceding discussion they lack conviction. Conversely, certain theological passages may be beautiful to read, but something is lacking if their everyday applications are ignored. If God speaks to us through the Scriptures, surely it is a matter of some importance that we receive the message in all its fullness.

There is another consideration. God's word is addressed to us for our salvation. What we sometimes forget is that this gift of salvation often runs counter to our own perceptions and expectations. The disposition that makes us capable of receiving salvation includes a willingness to be guided and to be changed.

Of our own free choice we entrust ourselves to the book we are reading. We come to it defenseless and ready to be influenced. This has something to say about the content of our reading: what books are suitable for *lectio divina*. We will have more to say about this later. The point we wish to examine at the moment is this sense of commitment. We open ourselves to the text, we approach it in a spirit of faith and obedience, ready to perceive in what we read the word of God, the will of God, the action of God coming to save us. This is the sort of book that is suitable for *lectio divina*. We approach our reading as a disciple comes to a master: receptive, docile, willing to be changed.

This means, in the first place, that we cannot afford to be too selective about what we encounter. God's saving of us takes place by dragging us beyond our own comfort zone into new territory and new adventures. It is an act by which we are drawn or even compelled to leave behind the boundaries that our selfhood has imposed upon our lives. We are called to transcend our own limited vision of the good life and to accept something of the all-inclusiveness of God's plan for human fulfillment. The greatest enemy to this is our own willful refusal to budge beyond the closed circuit of our settled prejudices and pious routines. *Lectio divina* is one concrete means of opening ourselves to the action of grace and the inspiration of the Holy Spirit.

This means that we have to stop trying to control the process. We have to take the risk of reading what is before us, allowing it to speak to our hearts and consciences and to cause us to look in a direction we had previously ignored. Self-programming is out of the question. Choosing our reading with too much precision is like playing tapes and never listening to the radio. We have the comfort of listening to our particular favorites whenever we want, but our exposure to new music is minimal. If we limit our reading to what we know from past experience, then we are in a rut and there is less likelihood that God's word will ever deliver us from our subjective prejudgments. Look at the cases where the Bible is used to legitimate persecution or discrimination. Those involved are not extracting a message from the sacred text. Instead they project their own message onto the words of Scripture and by frequent repetition convince themselves that the Bible thinks as they do. The Bible is an instrument of salvation only because it challenges our habitual beliefs, attitudes, and behavior. As soon as it begins only to confirm and reinforce our own views it is reduced to the status of a hand puppet. It no longer conveys an alternative; it simply parrots our own opinions.

It is the Bible's radically alternative viewpoint that we need to safeguard. In the early centuries this was a little easier in the sense that the term *lectio divina* was used to cover the public reading of the Scriptures. In such a situation, the choice of what was read was made by somebody else and the content of the reading had that quality of unpredictability that leaves room for God to surprise. In the monasteries, especially, the practice was always to have *lectio continua*, that is to say, the continuous reading of the Scriptures, carried on from day to day, omitting nothing. In this way honor was done to the integrity of revelation. No word inspired by God was dismissed by human beings as unsuitable for the task of enlightening those who heard it.

Needless to say, there are difficulties experienced in a method of reading that takes seriously the integrity of the text. Here our contemporary culture is no help. We are so obsessed with getting to the bottom line that we are inclined to short-circuit necessary preliminaries. As a result our understanding of the content is often approximate and superficial. We have lost the skill of tracking through a complex argument to arrive at unassailable conclusions. Instead we make a snap judgment and, to protect ourselves, leave our options open. We have lost the sense that sustained mental exercise is required to understand such ideas as the theory of relativity or the theology of the Eucharist. We are distrustful of anything that cannot be said plainly. As a result politicians are expected to summarize complex policies in a slogan or a thirty-second sound bite. Experts in various fields are lured onto television talk shows and required to reduce their life's labor into five minutes of moronic simplicity. Like children who need their food cut up for them, we prefer to deal with little pieces rather than to chew over complex issues for ourselves. If we wish to be nourished directly by the Scriptures without seeking a predigested substitute, then we will probably need to develop new skills.

The first requirement is patience. In fact, we have to slow down our intellectual metabolism and not expect to find quick and easy solutions to all life's problems. It is precisely this damping down of superficial excitement that creates the environment in which we are able to perceive spiritual things more intensely. It is like entering a cave. We need to give our eyes time to adjust to the dimmer light. In the same way, we who are so engrossed by the manifold concerns of daily living need to dull our surface sensibilities in order to become more aware of a level of reality that habitually evades our attention. Wanting to grasp everything immediately is the best way to comprehend nothing. We need time to adjust our rate of being to a more plodding pace and move slowly into a different ambience. We will talk about practical ways of doing this in a later chapter. Here the point is that sometimes a longer, more diffuse reading gives us more opportunity to make the transition into the spiritual zone than using a shorter, more focused text.

In some senses the medium is the message. What are we doing in *lectio divina*? We are seeking God. We are hoping to hear God's voice and do God's will, but we are operating in search mode. We have not yet attained the goal of our ambition, and so our reading is fundamentally an expression of our desire for God. We are aware that God is not fully present to us – or that we are not fully present to God. It is this sense of divine absence that makes us search more diligently. Authentic reading, therefore, has the character of dissatisfaction; we always want to go further and deeper. As pilgrims, seeking may be more truthful for us than finding. In our practice of *lectio divina,* a patient receptivity may serve us better than a clamorous urgency to be enlightened.

In an era of hyperstimulation it can be difficult for people to realize that enlightenment comes not by increasing the level of excitement, but by moving more deeply into calm. There is a kind of monotony that is not boredom but paves the way for a more profound experience. Those who approach *lectio divina* in the hope of a fireworks display will usually be disappointed. Sacred reading is not merely a form of pious entertainment. Its aim is to confront us with the truth of our own existence, and to accomplish this it has to break down all the barriers that we interpose between our awareness and the truth. We have to move to a level that is different from the one on which we operate in everyday life.[4]

Such a transition is not quickly effected. Our reading, like our prayer, mirrors the quality of our life. The exercises themselves are no more than the tip of the iceberg. We can fiddle with their formulas if we like, but no substantial improvement is likely. The major determinant of prayer or *lectio* is our fidelity to seeking God in everyday behavior. It is no good being fervent in reading if we are slack in living. On the other hand, we are more likely to be attuned to the message of the Gospels if our conduct is patterned according to evangelical priorities. Understanding the Gospels presupposes some attempt to live them. Neither goal is realized as quickly as we would like.

From all that we have been saying, it seems obvious that *lectio divina* is a sober, long term undertaking and, as such, better reflected in sustained attention to whole books than in seeking a quick fix from selected texts. There is no guarantee of immediate gratification at the level of experience or of immediate improvement in the quality of life. *Lectio divina* is an element in a lifelong process of turning toward God: its effects are discernible only in the long term. Equally, the effects of the absence of *lectio* may not be apparent to us until it is too late.

This patience is threatened by any kind of intellectual fascism. We cannot hear what a text is saying if we refuse to listen. And increasingly, many are reluctant to listen to truths or opinions that challenge any aspect of their personal view of reality. One of the failures of Western education is that it has not equipped people to read objectively books with which they disagree or about which they may have reservations.[5] There are those, for instance, who dismiss Saint Paul as a misogynist – and this sometimes on the basis of texts which, in the opinion of experts, Paul never wrote. If our convictions are so fragile that they cannot be exposed to alternative visions, then *lectio divina* is not for us.

Reading the Scriptures is the opposite of self-programming or any kind of brain washing. It is allowing God to speak to our hearts, minds, and consciences. While it is true that not every text will touch us each time that we read it, this does not justify our restricting ourselves to texts with known effects. The way out of an impasse is habitually surprising; if there were a familiar and easy exit, it would not be an impasse. Liberation is often a matter of tapping into previously unused potential, of transforming objects into assets. Guidance often comes from unlikely sources, as the Bible's own story of Balaam's ass reminds us (Numbers 22:28–30).

Once we have discerned an attraction for a particular book we should persevere with it. Maybe, like marathon runners, we will come up against a wall that seems to block any progress. This is the time when we need to trust that a choice made in good faith will not be fruitless and stay with it a little longer. Sometimes we are not ready for a particular inspiration immediately; in that case, our having to wait is one factor in slowly modifying our point of view. Oddly, it is often the experience of being blocked and frustrated that changes things by making us look in another direction for a solution.

An interesting saying is attributed to Abba Poemen, one of the desert fathers. On being asked to speak about the means of arriving at singleness of purpose, he replied:

> The nature of water is soft, that of stone is hard; but if a bottle is hung above the stone, allowing the water to fall drop by drop, it wears away the stone. So it is with the word of God; it is soft and our heart is hard, but the [one] who hears the word of God often, opens his heart to the fear of God.[6]

Water can wear away rock, but it needs time as its ally. God's word will certainly refashion our lives, but not overnight. The process begins from the center and works outward; its results will not be apparent on the surface for a very long time. Meanwhile, we have to accept and submit to the vagaries of this invisible process without losing heart or abandoning our sense of purpose.

Inevitably we will meet with obscurities in the text that have nothing to do with our subjective dispositions. We will be addressing some of these difficulties later in this book. The fact is that the Bible is an anthology whose contents derive from a period of more than a thousand years, are compiled in different languages, make use of different styles, and were written for different reasons. The Bible is inherently obscure for us; we have to work reasonably hard to extract meaning from the text. Most of us have to make do with a translation and that is another barrier to the direct contact between reader and writer that makes a book sparkle. We can expect some measure of difficulty in reading the Scriptures and need not be discouraged by it. The benefits of spending time with the Bible far outweigh the labors of coming to grips with its foreignness.

We can gain some encouragement from the example of the ancient monks. With hand-copied texts it was very hard to be sure of the accuracy of what one was reading. There was little in the way of internal division to facilitate referencing.[7] Commentaries were rare and not always informed. And it was not usually possible to have access to more than one book at a time. This meant that the monk reading the Gospels, for example, had to puzzle out for himself why the genealogy of Jesus is different in Matthew and Luke. His faith in the truthfulness of revelation invited him to read actively, to ask questions, to seek solutions – to search for a level of truth that was beneath the surface.

Staying with a single book is not only an exercise in personal discipline; it is a condition for approaching *lectio divina* with an appropriate attitude. It is not necessary that we understand all the reasons why this is important. Practice will reveal how sensible the tradition is. Meanwhile, if this is not our current practice, it is perhaps worthwhile to make an experiment to see whether this does not enhance our reading. We should be convinced, however, that the monastic practice favored a continuous reading of a single book, the *lectio continua*.

Here are some contrary ways of reading the Bible. In my view they fall short of the ideal of *lectio divina*. It seems to me that they lack the essential quality of openness to the unexpected that is such a feature of the traditional practice. Such approaches are better than nothing and *may* possibly be useful for beginners. For those who wish to be led further, however, it is probably wiser to re-examine one's priorities.

The Bible as medicine chest. At the end of the Gideon Bible, often left in hotel rooms and other places, there is a list of symptoms, each with a corresponding biblical text to remedy the situation. Are you depressed? Read such a text. Do you feel lonely? Read this one. This view of the Bible as a medicine chest seems to limit God's word to a merely instrumental role. We remain in charge. We diagnose the situation and then read the appropriate text. It may be that the scriptural passage indicated does offer us comfort and challenge. The danger is that we remain very much interred in our own assessment of our status.

Sometimes salvation is a matter of turning our own self-judgments inside out, not reinforcing them. The key to this possibility is often the addition of a new and hitherto unrecognized element into our view of the situation, the establishment of a link previously overlooked. The reading of familiar texts, especially if they are sought solely for comfort, does not have such an effect. No radical change of horizon has been effected.

"Cutting the Bible." In some circles a practice has developed of "cutting the Bible." This consists in letting the book of the Scriptures fall open at random and reading the first passage that catches the eye. In this case, the "responsibility" for what is read is transferred to God. There are some notable precedents for this practice including Saint Augustine, as he tells us in the story of his conversion. I can admit that in certain extraordinary and grave situations it is valid to tempt Providence in this way. However, it needs to be recognized that in many cases there is more than a tinge of superstition involved in such an approach. Furthermore, no effort is made to locate what is read in its own setting; it takes its context from the reader's situation, and this implies a step away from accepting that the text has an objective meaning.

Grazing. More common is an aimless meandering through the pages of the Bible, reading some bits, skipping over others, often leaving aside what is unfamiliar or obscure. Sometimes such undisciplined grazing yields nourishment for the spiritual life. More often it leads to a sense of boredom with the Bible that causes it effectively to be left aside. I have noted that persons who read regularly but haphazardly are often familiar with less than ten percent of the Bible. They know a few passages and occasionally resort to them, but progressively even these lose their charm. This lack of interest and commitment cannot sustain the effort and intensity needed for genuine *lectio divina*; the practice itself quickly collapses unless it is propped up by guilt or some external buttressing.

Liturgical reading. There are many people whose fidelity to reading the Bible takes the form of meditating daily on the texts read in the liturgy. This excellent practice often enhances participation in worship and injects into each day an element of personal encounter with God's word. It transfers the selection of passages away from one's own control and follows the guidance of the liturgy. This much is good. If this habit combines with a more continuous reading of Scripture, there will be many surprises at the number of "coincidences" that occur; the same message is often conveyed by different channels. In such cases personal reading and attention to liturgical texts are mutually enlightening.

What is restricting in following the texts of the missal, unsupported by other scriptural reading, is that one is materially limited to the excerpts used in worship, many of which lose some of their freshness through over-exposure. The problem is compounded when the text is edited or the translation used in the lectionaries is flat and unappealing. Furthermore, reading a preordained slab each day means that the rhythm of *lectio* is dictated by the liturgical cycle and less easily responds to personal attraction. Sometimes our personal situation means that we need to cover more distance to find nourishment; at other times a single sentence may keep us occupied for days. To reach the full depth of *lectio divina* we must learn to be led by our own attractions and to stay with them for as long as they exercise their fascination over us. It might be argued that it is more convenient simply to follow the liturgical cycle. This is undeniable. What I am saying is that the traditional practice of personal *lectio divina* was not so; it was a matter of remaining with whole books and reading them in their entirety over a prolonged period.

Texts in sequence. A person making an individually directed retreat is often given for reflection a sequence of scriptural texts. Sometimes these follow a pre-established schema, at other times they are chosen from session to session to correspond with the data emerging as the retreat progresses.

I find something a little manipulative about this practice. The Bible can be made to say what the director believes should be said without reference to any intrinsic meaning a text might have. I am aware that many benefit from this sort of thing, but it seems to me that for those who believe in the integrity of revelation this practice must raise certain doubts. Assuredly God can write straight on crooked lines, but why not try to draw straighter at the outset? This is especially true of people who have never come to terms with the Bible as a whole. For those who enjoy a familiarity with the totality of Scripture there is less danger. In such cases it can be helpful to be reminded of particular texts at different points in one's journey, so long as individual texts remain inserted in the total context of revelation. Any particular passage must carry in its wake other texts that complement and qualify its meaning. Without this broader reference, there is a lurking danger of subjectivism on the part either of the director or of the person making the retreat. God's word deserves to be heard in its own right and in its integrity and not merely used as a diagnostic agent or a means of persuasion towards an already decided goal.

Any personal encounter with God's word in Scripture is good and has power to change our lives for the better. If, however, we desire to make such reading a regular part of our lives we will probably find it helpful to manipulate the process as little as possible: to let God speak to us and to act on our hearts rather than to prescribe for ourselves the remedies we believe will make us better.

If we are going to follow Saint Benedict's recommendation and read biblical books in their entirety we will need to be prepared for a prolonged exposure to a particular book. If we choose to read the prophet Jeremiah or the Gospel of John, for instance, we can expect that either of these will fill the time available for *lectio* for three to six months. Our selection of material for *lectio* is something of an adventure. It is like choosing a companion for a long journey. In the months ahead I am going to be spending of lot of time in the other's company; my experience of the journey will be modified by my choice of companion. In the same way, six months spent in the company of the prophet Jeremiah gives me a different perspective on the events of my own life, and perhaps a new picture of the way God acts in our regard. It is not so much a question of a sudden revelation, but a gradual process of seeing things in a different light, much influenced by my fellow-traveller. Just as visiting an art gallery is a more wonderful experience in the company of an enthusiastic expert, so living beside Jeremiah or one of the other great spiritual giants slowly awakens us to the perception of spiritual reality latent in all that surrounds us. It changes our life in the sense that we begin to see things that were previously invisible, and this nuances our assessment of situations and often dictates new ways of responding to them.

There is much to be said in favor of this interpersonal aspect of *lectio divina*. Certainly it is a matter of making contact with the word of God, but this always happens through the intervention of other human beings. God does not speak directly, but inspires sages, prophets, and apostles who express in imperfect language the message they have perceived. It is not right to separate the content of the communication from its carrier. The inspired authors are not mute messengers. Just as it could almost be said that spending time with persons of quality is far more important than anything they might say to us, so there is more contained in the biblical books than the overt content. Beyond the message is the "meta-message."[8] The fact that God speaks to us at all is an indication that we are not considered by God to be beyond the pale of redemption.

Lectio divina involves allowing ourselves to be led to God by an experienced guide. Our attitude toward the author who acts as our mentor is one of openness, trust, and confidence. A friendship develops that is of great utility for us. For such a rapport to exist there must be prolonged contact. William of St Thierry, a twelfth-century Cistercian, noted this necessity.

> The Scriptures need to be read and understood in the same spirit in which they were created. You will never enter into Paul's meaning until, by good intention in reading and diligent zeal in meditating, you drink of his spirit. You will never understand David, unless by experience you clothe yourself with the feelings expressed in the psalms. And so for the other books. In all Scripture, diligent reading is as far from superficial perusal as friendship is distinct from acquaintance with a stranger, or as affection given to a companion differs from a casual greeting.[9]

Making friends with the author of our text demands that we really try to hear what is being said as distinct from what we would expect to be said. No friendship is possible without listening; we need to accept the other as distinct from ourselves and our projections and expectations. Only then can a friend be a source of vitality for us. With such an attitude, time increases our appreciation of the other and in the process we are changed.

Once we accept that we will be spending months with a particular book of the Bible, it seems prudent that we consider carefully our choice of reading. Sometimes people ask for a reading list – as though there were a "right" sequence to be followed. In reality, the choice of books is a very personal one, like the choice of friends.

In making our selection we are, to some extent, determining our future. Nobody else can do it for us. As we draw near to the end of our current text, we should reflect on where our attractions lie. If we have access to suitable people we might seek counsel. It is good to be very realistic about this decision, to take into account our present situation, our energy levels, our likely future demands. Sometimes some alternation is good; from Old Testament to New Testament, from John to Paul, from short book to long book. As far as possible we should combat the prospect of our getting into a rut, at the same time ensuring that we can commit ourselves to the book that we select. If feasible, we may find it useful to prepare the ground for *lectio* by some preliminary study. In a later chapter we will be looking at some practical suggestions in greater detail.

So the first challenge that monastic tradition offers to our current practice of *lectio divina* is to commit ourselves to sustained exposure to a single book. This is not as easy as it may seem. Hence some complementary issues need to be addressed.

Fidelity

The concept of *lectio divina* is more familiar today than it was thirty years ago. I doubt that there has been a corresponding increase in the quality of its practice. Even among monks and nuns the situation sometimes leaves something to be desired. I know for myself that to maintain fidelity to regular *lectio* is really very difficult.

Perhaps it would be useful to remind ourselves of some of the factors that make it a struggle. Here it is not a matter of assigning blame but simply of trying to understand why it can be difficult to sustain a routine of worthwhile *lectio divina*. By diagnosing the cause of present difficulties, perhaps we may be able to plan strategies for an improved future.

External difficulties. This can include noise, weather, constant unplanned interruptions, lack of books (though this is more common in the young churches that use a minority language), a general absence of tranquillity, age, ill health, a degree of dyslexia, or some passing or semipermanent anxiety. Such impediments are external; they are independent of the will. The situation can be modified sometimes by imaginative action, but mostly those in such circumstances will find it almost impossible to give themselves to *lectio* in the measure they would wish. In such cases it is a matter of submitting to the concrete exigencies of divine Providence and making the most of an undesirable situation.

Work, play, and other activities. We all need to work, play, study, talk to other people, attend meetings, eat, sleep, and be merry. None of these endeavors is compatible with quiet reflection on the Scriptures. When the sum total of these activities begins to occupy most of every day, then little time is left for personal reading. Inadvertently, without malice or forethought, *lectio divina* can be excluded from our daily occupations. This is a situation which asks us to review our priorities. Probably we can take realistic steps to improve the situation. We will have a little more to say about this later.

Good habits lost in time of change. For many religious especially, the last twenty-five years have witnessed considerable changes in basic values and lifestyle. As a result, those who are now middle-aged often have not yet developed the stable habits of prayer and *lectio* that one would expect of people of their seniority. This is not to accuse them of infidelity or neglect. They are not malefactors; they are the victims of the decades of turmoil, a generation caught unprepared by the demands of necessary (and desirable) change. Those of us whom Providence has placed in this situation, find ourselves obliged in mid-life to seek solid foundations that would more logically have been laid years ago.

Overexposure to words. Sometimes we feel that the Church is awash with words. Like the society in which we live, there is so much talk, so much paper, that even the liturgy is often threatened by verbosity. It is as though the volume of communication has outstripped its content, so that much of what is said is mere padding. To go beyond kindergarten level is considered elitist. As a result many who seek a more adult faith find it in withdrawal from wordiness into silence; quiet, objectless meditation seems preferable to the insincerity, banality, and ideological correctness that threaten to swamp the simplest message. To meet this objection we have first to recognize its validity. To solve the difficulty we have to insist that authentic *lectio*, far from being exposure to more mere words, is a means of setting aside the superficial to reach the heart of reality. It is the search for the unique Word of God who lies beneath and beyond the multiplied words of human beings.

Lack of training. In recent centuries the Church has expended considerable energy and resources in catechesis. There is great concern to ensure that the basics of Christian faith are fully and accurately presented. It seems that less attention is paid to those who have progressed beyond this elementary level. In the ancient Church catechetical instruction was supplemented by mystagogy (*mystagogia* – a leading into the mysteries). Today our catechesis produces such abundant fruit that there are many who desire to go further in the spiritual life, and whose attraction to do so comes from God. The tragedy is that there are few structures available to service this need. Many who pass through the Catholic school system are unaware of the strong mystical element in Christian tradition; if they later become interested in spirituality it is often outside the Church that they seek for guidance.

Sometimes our difficulty in facing up to a lifetime of *lectio* is simply a matter of not being trained for it. After an initial enthusiasm we feel ourselves blocked because no one has taught us where to go if we want to go further. The purpose of this book is to remedy this defect in some degree. In cases where people brought up with a facility for electronic media have a distaste for reading, an even more fundamental process has first to be initiated in which they are introduced or reconciled with books. Although tapes can be used by the visually impaired for *lectio*, I am not personally aware of any case in which the rhythm of genuine *lectio divina* has been reproduced by electronic means. Maybe in the future this will happen.

Boredom. Lack of training often leads to dissatisfaction with the results obtained in reading the Scriptures and so boredom quickly sets in. This is the situation where a person has leisure for reading the Bible and wishes to profit from it but is unable to get out of first gear. In other cases, what is described as boredom is more likely an impatience to finish *lectio* and to get back to doing something else that is more stimulating or rewarding. The experience of boredom is thus an indication that unconsciously the person wants to be somewhere else doing something different.

Negligence. Some difficulty in *lectio* is caused by our own slackness that leads us to abbreviate our reading or omit it altogether. Saint Benedict points to three particular enemies of *lectio divina* that lead to negligence: laziness, acedia, and fantasy.[10]

Laziness is an unwillingness to make an effort to do something that our mind approves. The causes for this reluctance are manifold; we are aware of some but others operate secretly. The bottom line is usually the same; we fail to take the steps that are possible which will lead to a better future. Acedia is a lack of commitment to spiritual values which leaves a person unable to settle down to anything serious for any length of time. Acedia has been recognized as the prevailing vice of Western society – symbolized perhaps by the remote control device for television. We all know people who seem unable to settle on any program. Those afflicted with this malady often cannot stay still to read; or alternatively, cannot give their attention to one book; they keep changing from one to another and instead of finding God are confronted only with their own restlessness.[11] Fantasy, whether it is a matter of escapist reading or entertainment, daydreaming or mindless conversation, is a voracious devourer of time. It poses a real threat to the possibility of spending some of our leisure time in openness to God's word. We all need to escape from the pressures of life sometimes, but many of us would be surprised if we calculated just how much of our day is dominated by such meaningless pursuits. I am not suggesting that we can live without frivolity. All I am saying is that if we need to make time for prayer and *lectio*, it can often be found by trimming such activities. The other problem associated with fantasy is that it often leads us away from truth and reduces our capacity to discern what is of permanent value and what is merely ephemeral. One who spends a disproportionate time in computer games, pulp novels[12] or watching television[13] may experience a certain debasement in the powers of the mind.

Such activities seem to leave a residue which sometimes subverts the concentration necessary for deep prayer or *lectio divina*. Not only does an addiction to unreality undermine our application during reading, it also makes us slow to begin, quick to finish, and reluctant to carry away from the exercise material for rumination. Our own mental wanderings become more comfortable and less challenging than the truth.

Duty. We all know situations where religion is used to keep God at a distance. Among those who are committed to the Scriptures, it is possible to develop a style of reading that defeats the purpose of the exercise. We can spend time with the Bible on a daily basis, read it closely and think about it, without really allowing God's word to wash over our conscience or to interact with the practical realities of everyday life. We are punctilious in observing our pious routine, but perfunctory in our efforts to go beyond the superficial layers of our being. Such usage honors God with the lips while the heart remains at a distance. We use our head, but consciences are untouched. A sense of duty brings us to the Bible and keeps us there, but there is little likelihood that such reading will ever revolutionize our lives.

These are some of the difficulties that (I know from my own experience) bedevil our efforts to give ourselves seriously to the practice of *lectio divina*. It is not a question of assigning blame for the inevitable slippage that comes in the course of a normal life. There are tactics that can help us: a bit of reorganization and a more realistic assessment of the demands on our time can sometimes create space where none seemed to exist. There is also the question of subjective disposition. This is where we can experience in our attraction to a greater exposure to God's word, a call to greater fidelity. Perhaps we need to be a little more faithful and a little more faith-filled, to give greater amplitude to our response of faith.

Assiduity

The word we often find in monastic tradition in connection with the practice of *lectio divina* is *assiduitas*, assiduity. This is an unusual noun in English which Roget associates with application, concentration, and intentness, although the Latin original has connotations more in the direction of constancy, continuity, perseverance. Applied to *lectio divina*, it seems to indicate that continuance in the practice is by no means automatic; many of us are intellectually convinced of its value, have good experience with it and yet easily find ourselves slipping away from its practice. And so we have to make an effort if we are to remain faithful to *lectio* throughout life.

There are four aspects of this notion of assiduity that can be of practical assistance to us in getting down to the job. I shall say a little about each.

Making time. You will notice that I do not say "finding time." For most of us there is no time lying around waiting to be discovered. If we want to include something worthwhile in our daily routine then we have to squeeze it in at the expense of other useful, desirable, or seemingly necessary activities. This involves two things. First, I have to accept responsibility for my own use of time and to stop regarding myself as the mere plaything or victim of external contingencies. Second, I have to take the trouble to establish some priorities about life. Inevitably this will mean that some gratifying employments may be reduced. So be it. I am the one setting the priorities; nobody else is to blame.

Lectio divina demands a solid commitment of time. The process is void if it is confined to spasmodic periods of no more than a few minutes. To generate its specific results it requires a certain density of experience – especially at the beginning of the journey. It is like the idea of the critical mass in nuclear physics: without a certain quantity of fissionable material no chain reaction follows. The formation of mind and heart that is due to *lectio divina* is realized only after a solid investment of time. I am thinking, for example, of a near-daily slot of about thirty minutes continuing over several years. This is a minimum level of commitment in average situations. I am aware that this may seem exigent and even impossible in particular cases, but I think it is worthwhile to be specific at this point. Commitment to spiritual progress by the way of *lectio divina* is unrealistic if, in practice, we cannot or will not allocate sufficient time. It is like learning a foreign language. Wanting to speak it is no substitute for regular exercise. Good excuses may absolve us from moral blame, but they don't help us to achieve the goal we set before ourselves.

I have found useful for myself the distinction between tasks that are urgent and those that are important. It is sometimes easy to give most of one's attention to activities that brook no delay. If we respond only to demands, we will often feel frustrated that we cannot be more creative in dealing with things that really matter. In such a case, the urgent and unimportant activity has squeezed out the important matter that is less pressing. Some activities are vital for continuing health, even though it makes little difference whether they are done today or tomorrow. The danger is that postponing something until tomorrow often becomes an unfulfilled promise. Many insoluble crises are simply the result of years of procrastination; important tasks left undone because they are not urgent eventually trigger an emergency of such scope that intervention is no longer possible.

I consider that *lectio divina* is an important component of the mature and active years of the spiritual life; its absence diminishes the vitality of these years and may eventually lead to shipwreck. Our efforts to establish priorities in our life will be smoother, perhaps, if we recognize that *lectio divina* has the right to be considered an important activity, even though its occasional omission makes little difference.

Regularity. Abbot Chapman of Downside has an incisive passage about regularity in one of his letters. He is writing about prayer, but the same principle is valid for *lectio divina*.

> The only way to pray is to pray; and the way to pray well is to pray much. If one has no time for this, then one must at least pray regularly. But the less one prays the worse it goes.[14]

We need the regular investment of energies if we are to hope for any appreciable harvest. There is a long passage in a sermon of Cardinal Newman that makes the same point eloquently.

> Now the duty of having stated times of private prayer is one of those observances concerning which we are apt to entertain the unbelieving thoughts I have been describing. It seems to us to be a form, or at least a light matter, to observe or omit; whereas in truth, such creatures are we, there is the most close and remarkable connexion between small observances and the permanence of our chief habits and practices. It is easy to see why it is irksome; because it presses upon us and is inconvenient. It is a duty which claims our attention continually, and its irksomeness leads our hearts to rebel; and then we proceed to search for reasons to justify our dislike of it. Nothing is more difficult than to be disciplined and regular in our religion. It is very easy to be religious by fits and starts, and to keep up our feelings by artificial

> stimulants; but regularity seems to trammel us and we become impatient. This is especially the case with those to whom the world is as yet new, and who can do as they please. Religion is the chief subject which meets them, which enjoins regularity; and they bear it only so far as they can make it like things of this world, something curious, or changeable, or exciting.

A later section of the same sermon demonstrates something of the vehemence of Newman's views in this matter. Abandoning due regularity is the beginning of a slippery slope that finally leads away from all authentic religion.

> When you have given over the practice of stated prayer, you gradually become weaker without knowing it ... Men first leave off private prayer; then they neglect the due observance of the Lord's day (which is a stated service of the same kind); then they gradually let slip from their minds the very idea of obedience to a fixed eternal law; then they actually allow themselves in things which their conscience condemns; then they lose the direction of their conscience, which being ill used, at length refuses to direct them. And thus, being left by their true inward guide, they are obliged to take another guide, their reason, which by itself knows little or nothing about religion; then this their blind reason forms a system of right or wrong for them, as well as it can, flattering to their own desires, and presumptuous where it is not actually corrupt ... Such is the course of disobedience, beginning in (apparently) slight omissions, and ending in open unbelief ...[15]

Saint Benedict insists that the monk's day includes definite times for reading.[16] This is to say that such periods are known in advance, they are not subject to whim, they can be somewhat protected from thoughtless intrusion. In addition, a good routine means that we give ourselves to *lectio* as a matter of course. It is built into whatever structure we have in our day or week. We do not have to endure the drama of making decisions, but rather move into it on automatic pilot, as it were. This priority is apparent in William of St. Thierry's *Golden Epistle*, which we have already quoted.

> At specified times, room should be made for specific reading, for the casual and random reading of whatever comes to hand is not constructive. On the contrary it upsets the mind. And whatever finds an easy entrance to the mind is as easily lost. It is better to

> spend a good deal of time with particular authors and so let your mind get used to them.[17]

Another good effect of having a regular time slot is that the particular time chosen begins to have its own character. It becomes sacred time for us and our efforts to pray or read during this period are more fruitful. Good habits are built up by the repetition of good acts; once good habits have taken root they make it easier to perform good, and as a result we get more for our pains.

An aspect of regularity that Thomas Merton makes much of in his work *Inner Experience* is making use of Sunday.[18] One of the creative things that we could do is to attempt to restore to Sunday something of its sacred character, and one of the ways of doing this could be to avail ourselves of the leisure it affords to spend some time in *lectio divina*. As it happens, this is also Saint Benedict's suggestion (RB 48.23).

Repetition. In the West we have become accustomed to a lineal logic; we begin at A and progress to Z. We keep pressing forward, never turning back. The art of sacred reading does not follow this pattern of inevitable forward movement. It certainly begins at the beginning and continues until the end, but there is much meandering in between. Repetition is the soul of genuine *lectio*. It is a right brain activity; we do not grasp the entire content immediately but in a circular manner. We read and advance, then we go back and read again. With each repetition, something new may strike us. Not only do we repeat books in the course of a lifetime, perhaps we re-read chapters and parts of chapters and even verses as a normal way of spending time with a text. We do not race ahead like a speed boat; our progress is like that of a minesweeper, crisscrossing the same places several times as we go forward. It takes time for us to become attuned to the subtle rhythms of a particular writing; the more we can slow down our reading, the more likely it is that we will catch sight of something unexpected.

The reading of a scriptural book is a little like painting a wall. We accept in principle that it is something that has to be done every few years; it can never be finished permanently. Probably we will use the occasion of repainting to change the color somewhat to correspond with current needs, and the result will create a new ambience in which to live. Two or three coats of paint are necessary to ensure total coverage of the wall, and in the process of applying each coat we move back and forth, sometimes going over what has already been done, sometimes moving into new territory. A lot of repetition and overlap is needed to achieve a smooth finish, but when all is complete, only the harmony of the finished product is visible. It is not a perfect image of *lectio divina* but it does highlight its circular rather than lineal character.

Perseverance. Since *lectio divina* is a long-term project it will probably do us little good if we do not persevere in its practice. Spasmodic bursts are not enough. This means that we need a sense of dedication and commitment, as well as the practical nous to translate these into behavioral realities. Many people who give up prayer or *lectio* often give as their reason, "I don't get anything out of it." Sometimes we all feel this way, but it is important to keep up our practice when the going gets tough – perhaps also seeking counsel to understand better what is happening.

Perseverance needs to be worked at. This means that we have to monitor our performance from time to time. At a time of retreat, for example, it is worthwhile assessing how well our good intentions have been realized. It may be useful for some to make a diary entry – either to ensure that time is allocated or to check whether we are, in fact, living according to our priorities. We who are so professional in other spheres of our lives can sometimes transfer some of our skills to support our devotional life. We do not have to be constantly monitoring our actions, but it is prudent for us to do so occasionally, especially if elements of our life sometimes get out of control.

I am aware that this section may seem harsh, prescriptive. and guilt-provoking. That is not my intention. I am primarily interested in providing tactics for the future rather than passing judgment on the past. Any effort that we make to improve inevitably dismisses present performance as less desirable. I do not doubt that most of us have been doing the best we could. I am not talking about the past. What I am saying is that the key to a better future is a solid commitment to spending time on a regular basis. That is the traditional wisdom and, on the basis of my own limited experience, I have found that it is true.

Of course if we think of *lectio divina* only in terms of duty, obligation, and struggle, its continuing practice will be a burden for us and we will experience all kinds of psychological resistance to it. In fact, once we overcome our reluctance and get stuck into it, we will find sacred reading to be a positive element in our lives; a source of energy, direction, and vitality. The problem is, as Dietrich Bonhoeffer used to insist, there is no cheap grace. To experience the joy inherent in this great gift of God we have to pay our dues. This involves a substantial, open-ended investment of time and effort and the willingness to trust the experience of others when we are assured that it is all worthwhile.

Reverence

The fourth characteristic emphasis to be found in the benedictine tradition is on the spirit of reverence that should pervade our reading. Reverence is an attribute much appreciated in the sober tradition of which Saint Benedict was a part.[19] It is a value that is not much addressed in Western culture, nor does it seem to rank very highly in the catechesis.

What is reverence before God? It is the sobriety of spirit that stems from an experience of the otherness of God which makes us want to subdue self, remain silent, and to submit. We are overwhelmed by the greatness of God present and are reluctant to spoil the occasion by the intrusion of our own fatuity. Reverence is what Job experienced when the Lord intervened to restore his fortunes (Job 42:1–6). When God is absent, human words and logic seem powerful and convincing. In the presence of God, however, such credibility melts: Job recognizes the foolishness of what he had been saying and withdraws into a silence that is more full of content than any of his windy discussions. Reverence is closer to awe than to fear. It is the recognition of a presence that is larger than oneself.

In the Eastern Church there is a strong tradition of *apóphasis* or negation. God cannot be described adequately in positive terms, but only by denying to God any human concept that includes limitation. Thus God can be said to be timeless, immutable, beyond imagination. God cannot be said to have color or gender or to inhabit a particular place – except by way of analogy. We demonstrate the depth of our knowledge of God when we affirm the divine unknowability. The apophatic tradition calls us to accept God as a totality that is beyond our comprehension, to be humble before the mystery of God. It is this humility that is the key to unlocking the depths of revelation.

It is reverence that makes us assiduous and persevering in our exposure to God's word. We recognize the limitations of an existence without God and we want to provide as many openings as possible for God to enter our life and to influence our living of it. Let us examine five ways in which the spirit of reverence shapes *lectio divina*.

First, reverence propels us toward silence, and silence enables us to listen. If we are to live according to God's word we must first hear what is said. That usually involves the labor of listening. *Lectio* is the time to leave aside other thoughts and concerns and to devote ourselves entirely to sitting at the Lord's feet and allowing ourselves to be instructed. "It is appropriate for the teacher to speak and teach; the disciple is to be silent and listen."[20]

Secondly, reverence will cause us to surround our reading with safeguards to its seriousness. This means a certain amount of care expended in the choice of time and place, attention to the quality of the environment in which our *lectio* is done. I believe that it also involves honoring the book of the Bible. This means using it with a certain degree of formality: not scribbling on it or using it for profane purposes, but keeping it special. Many people find that a little ritual enhances the quality of sacred reading: an opening prayer, a particular posture, the use of flowers or candles or icons.

Thirdly, reverence for God's word means respect for the text of the Bible. On the one hand, this excludes the biblical jokes that are often made by professional religious persons. On the other, it points to a zeal for the authentic meaning of the text and a corresponding reluctance to twist the Bible's meaning to suit extrinsic demands. Not all of us have the full range of skills necessary to arrive at an expert opinion on the meaning of a particular text. All that reverence obliges is that we do our best to confront the bare word of God with as little prejudgment as possible. As we will see in the next chapter, we are not alone in this. The Bible is addressed not to me as an individual but as member of the Church. Often a hidden meaning will be unveiled only by recourse to a brother or sister.

It is also our reverence for the wonder of revelation that disinclines us to allow any moment of grace to slip away. Like Mary, the mother of Jesus, we cherish the word, pondering it in our hearts (Luke 2:19, 2:51). The process of reading the text is only a beginning; it is meant to lead us to a greater mindfulness. *Lectio divina* is incomplete if we do not carry away from it something to ponder. Again, William of St. Thierry's *Golden Epistle* addresses this matter.

> Some part of your daily reading should, each day, be stored in the stomach of memory and left to be digested. At times it should be brought up again for frequent rumination. You should select something that is in keeping with your calling and in line with your personal orientation, something that will seize hold of the mind and not allow it to think over alien matters.[21]

It is because we value what we read that we are reluctant to part with it. By retaining some level of contact we not only extract from the text all that it has to say to us, we also introduce into our day a unifying force that battles against the fragmentation occasioned by so many different demands on our attention.

The final quality that reverence builds in us is a determination to put into practice the good news encountered in *lectio* – to be not merely hearers of the word but doers. In many languages the words for "obedience" and "listening" are cousins, reminding us that we do not fully hear what God says unless we submit to it in daily life. This is what Saint Paul names the "obedience of faith" (Romans 1:5, 16:26). A spirit of obedience is needed not only after our *lectio*, but during it and before it. We need to approach our reading with an antecedent willingness to be called, challenged, converted. This abandonment of narcissistic control is one of the prime dynamics in sacred reading that leads us to more mature faith and a more fruitful humanity.

A spirit of reverence is an essential component of *lectio divina*; without it, reading the Scriptures becomes a trivial exercise of piety. Saint Caesarius of Arles (d. 542) strongly affirms this in a well-known passage:

> Brothers and sisters, here is a question for you: Which to you seems the greater, the word of God or the body of Christ? If you want to give the right answer you will reply that God's word is not less than Christ's body. Therefore, just as we take care when we

> receive the body of Christ so that no part of it falls to the ground so, likewise, should we ensure that the word of God which is given to us is not lost to our souls because we are speaking or thinking about something different. One who listens negligently to God's word is just as guilty as one who, through carelessness, allows Christ's body to fall to the ground.[22]

Lack of reverence is an indication of deficient understanding and points to a certain grossness of mind that is unable to perceive the true nature of spiritual reality. It is unfortunately true that "familiarity breeds contempt," but this does not make flippancy concerning the great mysteries of our faith any more excusable.

One who has really grasped the magnitude of God's gift will be in awe of every aspect of the divine bounty. In some cultures there is a highly developed etiquette for receiving a gift: the fact of being remembered, the care for the formalities of handing it over, its wrapping – all are as much appreciated as the gift itself. They are all expressive of affection and esteem. In the same way, our reception of divine revelation is not merely a matter of extracting an orthodox theological conclusion and discarding the husks. There are many layers and levels of meaning which convey the same message in different but mutually reinforcing ways. *Lectio divina* teaches us to be zealous in welcoming the word and to cherish and celebrate the manifold revelation of God, incarnate in the Scriptures. Without reverence this is impossible.

Compunction

Reverence is a stable feeling, more or less uniform in its expression. The other attitudinal component of *lectio divina* is fanned into flame by fervent attention to the Scriptures. The term most often used in monastic tradition for the feeling that the Bible inspires in us is "compunction."[23] The word of God awakens in us our latent spiritual sense; we become aware of realities that, until this, had been forced below the threshold of our minds: God's call, our need for God, our desire to live a different kind of life. Compunction operates on the level of our feelings, but it is more than mere sentiment. Our feelings alert us to changes taking place at a much deeper level of our being, at the level of our heart.

It is by compunction that we discover what is happening in our own inner world. The text of Scripture becomes, as Saint Athanasius says, "a mirror in which may be seen the movements of one's own soul."[24] *Lectio divina* is not only a means of discovering something about God; it also helps us to understand our hidden selves. It is not the alienating absorption of a message that is foreign or even hostile to our own deepest aspirations; it is the surprising conclusion that our most authentic level of being is mirrored in the Scriptures. What is most intimate to our existence as persons is nourished and nurtured by God's word. What we feel in compunction is the fact that our whole being responds to the comfort and challenge of being addressed at a level that is commonly ignored.

The coloring of compunction varies. Sometimes it is bright and joyous, at others it seems somber and judgmental. In both cases the content of the experience is less important than the fact of it. To feel anything at all is a great relief if we have recently passed through long periods in which our practice of religion is marked only by numbness and blankness. In an estranged relationship anything is better than continuing coolness. Those whose religious enthusiasm declines during the years because "nothing ever happens" will take heart once God appears to speak to them again – even though the message may be a challenge to the status quo.

Renewed zest for *lectio divina* is one of the most powerful means of escaping from the limbo of feelinglessness. When our spiritual life loses its dynamic character we need to look around for a source of renewal that will reactivate our sensibilities by exposing us to something fresh. Fidelity to *lectio* is a means of allowing the formula of our life to adapt to changing circumstances so that we do not become stale and flaccid. After a period in which our personal discipline has – for one reason or another – become slack, the best way to start reversing the decline is to reinsert ourselves into regular *lectio*.

This outcome depends not only on the grace of God but also on our willingness to be touched. It means opening ourselves to a level of vulnerability that may be impossible at other times and in other activities. We come to the Scriptures aware that our souls are perishing through starvation and we allow ourselves to express our desire to be fed. This is not mere imaginative rhetoric. The "piety void" that many good people experience is both real and painful. It exposes their fragility and the wounds that life has inflicted on them. These are the matrix upon which the experience of *lectio divina* is formed. The Scriptures are not only food they are also medicine.[25] The experience of compunction during reading is a moment of high intensity that embraces not only the present; it has the capacity to heal the past and to fill us with energy for a more divine future.

This "devotional" aspect is not to be disdained. Living a spiritual life in obedience to the mandates of the Gospel involves considerable curtailment of options – the Christian is expected to abstain from a whole alphabet of vices from adultery to zoophilia. For most of us even the most minimal renunciation does not come easily unless there is some compensation at another level – or at least a realistic hope of it. To embrace the negative component of New Testament teaching we have to be sustained by the experience of some of its positive realities. It is true that if we have treasure in heaven, then we are less likely to be bowled over by earthly reverses (Matthew 6:21). It is also true that unless we have first discovered and in some way possessed that treasure we are totally unlikely to make the sacrifices involved in adherence to the kingdom (Matthew 13:44, 19:21). The point about *lectio divina* is that it not only enlightens the mind, it also massages the will – we usually need more help to do what we know should be done than to know what it is. Certainly, our dedication to sacred reading will bring us a greater familiarity with divine truth, but it does this in such a way that we are energized to embrace God's will and not merely informed of it. It is a matter of motivation rather than obligation. We are not merely told to "avoid evil and do good" (Psalm 34:14), we are given the incentive and desire to do so.

This has implications for the kind of space we create in which to read. It is not only a matter of taking up the sacred text with a mind that is cleared of trivial or unworthy preoccupations. We come with a will that is receptive and ready to be influenced. This is different from our normal reading. Mostly we read for information. *Lectio divina* operates more at the level of persuasion. Few of the books of the Bible were written with a view to conveying brute facts; facts are included, but only as instruments of motivation. If we are not willing to be wooed in our reading, the exercise will degenerate into mere foraging for information; it will not have the power to change our lives.

To have the courage to expose ourselves to influence we need to be convinced the outcome will be to our ultimate advantage. On occasion I have deferred opening a letter because I feared it brought bad news. There is no need to be so fearful about *lectio divina*: the Gospel is good news. However threatening it may appear at first sight, the word of God seeks only our well-being and joy. When our lives are glum, often it is because we have withdrawn from the joy and hope that stem from faith and, instead, allow ourselves to be overwhelmed by immediate problems.

The world of compunction is the world of sensibility to God. We allow God to act upon us not only by the medium of ideas but also through our feelings. Imagine how artificial a relationship between two persons would be if it involved only ideas: no sight or sound or touches. How difficult it would be, in those circumstances, to become passionate. Such a relationship would be so rarefied and abstract that it would lack reality – unless a different game were being played at the level of the unconscious. It is emotion that bonds us with other persons. And so, we cannot relate to God feeling nothing. On the contrary, our feelings can be indicators of God's action. Certainly there is scope for discernment and common sense, but it seems to me better to be a little mistaken in the diagnosis of the source of feeling than to attempt to live a spiritual life of substantial feelinglessness. In the providence of God, even our errors can sometimes be useful.

The monastic linkage of *lectio divina* and compunction is a reminder that there is more involved in sacred reading than intellectual stimulation.

2

THE THEOLOGICAL BASIS OF *LECTIO*

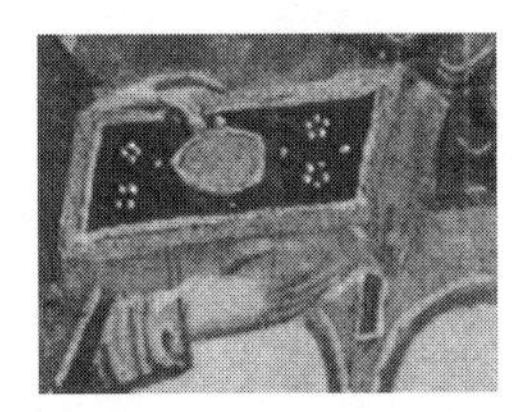

We find in monastic tradition an abundance of practical and tactical suggestions about the exercise of *lectio divina.* Before following these recommendations uncritically we need to know something about the reasons underlying them. Inevitably there are cultural and philosophical presuppositions, but the most important element of theory to be examined is the theology of Scripture reading. If we are to adopt and adapt some of the practices of medieval monasticism, we need to be sure that the theology on which they are based is sound.

Monasticism identified itself primarily in terms of an evangelical life, a serious response to the Gospel. It was not so much a mindless denial of the ways of the wicked world; it was more a matter of living according to the objective teaching of Christ. This was conveyed in the book of the Scriptures and the words of experienced elders. What Armand Veilleux has written of the Coptic monks was true more generally: "Holy Scripture was, for the Pachomian monk, the first – and in some measure the only – rule of his monastic life. It was, at the same time, the guiding inspiration of his spirituality."[1] Monks were, almost by definition, men of the book, and this is why they went to such trouble to preserve the biblical text, to purge it of mistakes, and to transmit to succeeding generations both the book and the skills to read it.

There are three important themes in a monastic theology of the Bible that can be helpful for us today. The first points to the role of *lectio* in leading us to prayer and ultimately to contemplation. The second emphasizes the corporate and ecclesial nature of revelation and offers us some protection against the idiocies of subjectivism. The third reminds us that God's word comes to us in earthen vessels and helps us to separate the gold from the dross.

The school of Christ

A wonderful sentence at the end of the Prologue to Saint Benedict's Rule refers to us as being recipients of the *magisterium* of Christ.[2] So long as our fervor remains intact we continue as learners. We are pupils in the school of the Lord's service, or, as the medieval Cistercians loved to say, we belong to the school of Christ. This image is not intended to emphasize our status as non-proficient – as though we were to remain immature all our lives. It means that as individuals and as members of a group, monks are striving to acquire only one skill – to learn Christ. What other desire is at the heart of the vocation of every fervent Christian man and woman?

Contact with God's word comes through the Church's proclamation, through reading the Scriptures and through the counsel of a graced elder. These conspire with deep inner processes to shape our conscience. Our willingness to listen and to be formed by God's word is what constitutes us as members of Christ's school. Although the primary focus of the Christian is necessarily the fourfold gospel, yet the full implications of the message of Jesus can be appreciated better still by reading them in the context of the New Testament and of the whole Bible. The traditional understanding was that every page of the Scriptures spoke about Christ – revealing to us the rhythms of God's plan for our salvation and the way we can increase our capacity to be open to it. The whole Bible can be viewed retrospectively as leading us to Christ, as Saint Paul says (Galatians 3:24), and this is why the ancients used to read and comment on the Old Testament in full awareness of what had been wrought in the New. As Saint Jerome said in a famous axiom, "Not to know the Scriptures is to be ignorant of Christ."[3]

The Word of God, incarnate in Jesus, also spoke at different times and in different ways through the Law, the Prophets, and the Writings (see Hebrews 1:1). Throughout the Bible the Revealer is one. This is why it can be said that in a certain sense it is Christ who speaks to us, in different ways, in all the different types of writing that make up the Bible. To be attentive to the Bible, for us Christians, is to listen to Christ, to be formed by him, to be called to follow him as disciples. The whole purpose of discipleship is to accept to be influenced. Whatever part of the Scriptures we read, Christ our teacher is waiting to instruct us. This is what the traditional Christocentric reading of the Bible means. We learn not only about Christ but from Christ.

We open the Scriptures to find Christ. The same is true of both Testaments. Reading the Bible is our means of expressing our discipleship; we come as willing learners to our master. This relationship may be said to pass through four phases.[4]

Following. First, we must implement what we hear. Disciples express their attachment to a master by following the injunctions given them. This means abandoning their own judgments and preferences and choosing to be governed by another – at least, to some extent.

Initially there are instructions or rules given by the master that the apprentice is expected to follow. These are prescribed according to the disciple's needs and stage of growth. Those who are more advanced, including the master himself, may be dispensed from them, but they remain binding on the disciple. In the first phases of apprenticeship, the disciple's task is simply to obey. At this moment the Christian takes the Gospels as a program of life and seeks to put into effect the teaching of Christ through obedience to what is read. Christ said, "Love your enemies" and "Have no care for tomorrow"; I shall try to practice these principles by active obedience. Progressively, however, the disciple follows not only what the master says, but also what the master does. This is to progress to the second stage.

Imitation. In the second phase, example is a more potent influence than verbal teaching. Sometimes imitation is unconscious. Without knowing it, a disciple may begin to mimic a mentor's style or mannerisms. What this sometimes amusing behavior indicates is that a bonding is taking place between disciple and master. The Christian disciple understands that there is more to following Christ than simply conforming to a series of objective instructions. It is a matter of living as Christ lived, acting as Christ acted.

The New Testament itself frequently exhorts us to this. The Gospels were written not only to give us information about the life of Jesus but also to present it to us as a model for imitation. This is especially true in the area of suffering. Jesus' response to pain and persecution is offered to us for guidance in our own difficult hours. The account of Jesus' prayer in Gethsemane, for instance, is meant to teach us how to act when we are confronted with the prospect of sorrow, aloneness, rejection, and death. It imprints on our awareness the example of Jesus so that when the hour comes we may have the resources to do as he did.

Likeness. Aspiring to likeness to Christ is an advance on merely repeating what Christ said or did; it is a matter of trying to be as Christ was. According to a common view among the Fathers of the Church, human beings created in the image of God have as their fundamental moral priority, to become like God. In Gospel terms, this is a matter of being perfect as God is perfect. Whatever our resources, whatever our situation, we are called to transcend our limitations and to become more like Christ. We gradually take on the task of being Christ's representative in our own setting: an icon of Christ for seekers of truth, a servant to those in need, a friend to the lonely, and even, as Saint Paul says, a source of scandal to those on the way to perdition.

Participation. Beyond likeness is identification. This is what is referred to in the well-known quotation from Galatians 2:20: "I live now, not I, but Christ lives in me." When Gregory of Nyssa (d. 395) says that "Christianity is an imitation of the divine nature,"[5] it is clear that he is not speaking at the level of moral choices and actions, but is referring to our innate participation in the divine being. Not only do we consciously speak, act, and present ourselves as "other Christs," but Christ works in us. The resulting action is more his than ours. Because of the mystical association, begun in baptism and deepened by grace throughout life, Christ is more truly identified as the subject of our good actions than we ourselves. Our Christian lives are not a matter of performing particular approved actions; they involve the renunciation of a private ethic in order to permit Christ's Spirit to be the source of all we do.

In these four stages we see how our point of contact with Christ is becoming more and more interior. From mere external obedience we progress to a point of participating in the subjectivity of Christ. There is, however, a price to pay for this transparency; it is necessary for our egotism to be diminished until it disappears. Christ's involvement in our action is inhibited by our self-centered concerns. Only when these are left aside is there much possibility of our actions becoming suffused with the power and presence of the risen Lord.

It is important for us to remember that entering into the subjectivity of Jesus Christ is the goal of Christian life. To be and to live "in Christ" – nothing less. Our prayer is to be a sharing of Jesus' own Spirit-filled movement towards the Father. Our daily life is a call to approach people in the power of Jesus' self-forgetful identification with their hopes and struggles.[6] Ideally our life is stamped with the character of Christ. We have received his Spirit. This means that we are given the opportunity to participate in the attitudes of Jesus: to have the mind of Christ, as Saint Paul says (Philippians 2:5, 1 Corinthians 2:16).

When our minds and hearts are formed according to Christ, then our actions can be vehicles of grace to others. The precondition is, however, that our consciousness is shaped to agree with that of Christ. And this is precisely the role of *lectio divina*. It is a school in which we learn Christ.[7] In any master–disciple relationship, the content of what is learned is less important than the relationship itself; it is prolonged mutual presence that communicates to the disciple the spirit and style of the elder. *Lectio divina* helps us to encounter Christ, it initiates us into the way of Christ. As many persons have said, in Christianity the Word of God is a person, not a book.

Lectio divina is an essential element in the flowering of contemplation. What is contemplation? It is a change in consciousness marked by two elements. On the one hand, there is a recession from ordinary sensate and intellectual awareness and all the concerns and programs that depend upon it. At the same time, more subtly, it is being possessed by the reality and mystery of God. Having emptied oneself in imitation of Christ (Philippians 2:7), one is filled with the fullness of God. "Of his fullness we have all received, grace for grace" (John 1:16).[8] The endowments of Christ become ours – in particular his relationship with the Father. In graced living Christ becomes the doer of our actions; in contemplation we become the subject of Christ's prayer. There is a mysterious interpenetration of subjectivity in the realm of supernatural existence.

Here it is important to introduce a necessary qualification. All that we are saying must be viewed in a corporate context. Despite the intensity of the experience, mystical union with God does not represent a narrowing of horizons so that nothing outside the self and God is taken seriously. Authentic mystical experience is inseparable from entry into a wider world; at its height it is all-inclusive. Union with God is experienced only on the condition that one is united to all the whole creation. This is the meaning of the double commandment: love God, love your neighbor. If *lectio* leads to contemplation, it must also be a progressive initiation into solidarity with all humanity.

A common inheritance

From the sixteenth century until the first half of the twentieth there was a tendency to emphasize the human being in isolation (the "individual") at the expense of the human being in relationship (the "person").[9] As a result, a number of false polarities have arisen in the sphere of people's relationship with the Church:

outer ⋊ inner

person ⋊ community

differences ⋊ similarities

freedom ⋊ authority

spontaneity ⋊ structure

devotions ⋊ liturgy

The result was a spirituality that was very interior; there was great emphasis on the vertical aspects (God and I) and a corresponding loss of sensitivity to corporate (horizontal) and corporal values. Such religion, as Counter-Reformation Catholics know well, often became dry, legalistic, institutional, with a tendency to rationalism. On the other hand, emotion, excluded from participation, degenerated into emotionalism and often became rampantly eccentric.[10] In such a context flourished sentimental devotion, pietism, subjectivism, and a tendency to the private interpretation of Scripture.

The priorities inherent in both extremes of this situation have been more recently reversed. The Church is less often viewed as a mere institution, except by those who, for their own purposes, wish to caricature it. The corporate elements of Christian life are more amply appreciated. Mostly this has come about as an instinctive reaction against a spirituality that was not producing the desired effects. However, the resulting network of values is often as unbalanced as the system it replaces. The danger we now face is that some important values that seemed self-evident in the past may become marginalized and even face extinction. Perhaps in the dialectic of history, future scholars may discover a movement toward synthesis. This can be of little comfort to us, who are living through the transition, if we have not achieved some harmonious blending of opposites in our own lives. We must remove spirituality and mysticism from the sphere of the individual and relocate them in an ecclesial context.

Lectio divina was originally the term used for liturgical readings and, as such, was necessarily communal. Because we employ the term principally to describe a personal encounter with God's word, it is more difficult for us to be aware of its essentially communal and ecclesial character. This is why an important part of our review of the theology that grounds the practice of *lectio* must be to recall the intrinsic relationship that exists between the Bible and the Church.

Mutuality exists between the Church and sacred Scripture. Historically the Scriptures were created, edited, preserved, disseminated, and explained by the Church. Without the Church there would be no Bible: it was not handed down from heaven on a silver platter, it is the product of the Church's inspired industry. At the same time, without the Bible there would be no Church. Without the proclamation of the good news in some form, oral or written, the Church would have no common faith to bind its adherents together. The Bible is the Church's constitutional text, its canon. The Church is the medium in which the Bible grew and outside which it cannot exist. Where there is Bible, to that extent there is Church; where there is Church, there in some form the Scriptures must be found. To use an ancient image, the Bible is an essential part of what the Church has inherited, part of its patrimony: it is the dowry of Christ's Bride. The Church cannot exist or act without this gift.

Both Scripture and the Church are expressions of the divine initiative for our welfare. Both are instruments by which God's saving act is made known to us. But they are more than that. They are also mysterious means by which we come into direct contact with the power of salvation. In other words, they are "sacraments" – using this term in the broad sense. The Scriptures and the Church do not merely inform us about God; they provide the means by which we become part of what we read about. The proclamation of salvation is interactive – to receive revelation is to participate in the mystery that is revealed. Scripture is not properly read except in the context of the Church as the primary sacrament of God's presence among us.[11] In fact, it is possible to define the Church as that ambience in which God's word is read, welcomed, pondered, and put into practice. We could also say that revelation is incomplete while it remains on the pages of a book. The purpose of God's word is to save all of us. Its work is incomplete until the end of time when God will be "all in all" (1 Corinthians 15:28). Until all the elect have received the word to the extent of their capacity, have made it their own and expressed it in love and celebration, the work of revelation is unfinished. Necessarily, then, the work of revelation continues in the life of the Church. Bible and Church are bound together.

On a practical level, this means that *lectio divina* is always an encounter with the Church as sacrament. Reading the Scriptures leads us towards the experience of the communion of saints and puts us in touch with the reality of the Church, both local and universal. As such, the Bible is a unitive force in the local community, in the universal Church and, one might say, throughout the world. To use the Scriptures merely as ammunition for polemic – either against unbelievers or, worse still, against those of the household of the faith – is contrary to the nature of God's gift.

The Church's mission to humanity is to facilitate access to God's word. This statement needs to be interpreted in a more-than-material sense. It is not enough for the Church to operate a printing press to ensure that everyone has a copy of the Bible. Access to the text is good, but often we need milk before we are ready for solid food (1 Corinthians 3:2). The Church mediates the Scriptures more amply by translating them into known languages, by helping us to understand the parts of Scripture in the context of the whole, by providing a doctrinal setting, and by sharing with us the fruits of the graced experience of two thousand years. In this way we are protected from erroneous first impressions (see 2 Peter 3:16–17) and set on the path to a growing understanding of what is being revealed.

The ecclesial context of *lectio divina* enhances its power for good. Our union with the Church helps us to be more integrally in contact with the revealed word. Christ and his Church are inseparable. There is a complementary truth. Our reading of the Scriptures contributes something to Church as a whole. Our measure of openness to God is a means by which divine revelation enters this world to save it. We become receptors of grace with the capacity of transmitting further what we ourselves receive. We read in union with the whole people of God and so our reading is a source of energy for the whole Church. Like the spreading carpet of light at the Easter Vigil, we accept our small measure of the light of Christ, we communicate it to another and soon the darkness is transformed into a thousand points of light. *Lectio divina* enables God's word to be born once more in our hearts and in our world. Who knows the good that will result from it?

The Fathers of the Church used to say of Mary, the mother of the Lord, that she was the receiver of God's word *par excellence*. She welcomed the Word in her mind before the Word became flesh in her body. In those secret months of cherishing and nurturing the Word, she became the model of the contemplative Church. Her words at the Annunciation might well be ours as we begin our *lectio*: "Behold the Lord's servant; let it be done to me according to your word" (Luke 1:38).

The "abbreviated word"

Our appreciation of the essentially ecclesial character of the revealed Scriptures protects us from eccentricity. The Bible belongs to the Church; we cannot, as individuals, claim mastery of it. Indeed, relatively few people have read the entire Bible and only a handful would even claim detailed knowledge of the totality. Ask a biblical exegete a question outside the sphere of his or her specialization and you will receive only a general and probably provisional answer. The entire content of revelation cannot be compressed into a synthesis: it is unwieldy and disparate. The longer one spends at the study of Scripture, the more convinced one becomes that one has scarcely progressed beyond the beginning.[12] If this is true of knowledge, it holds even more validity in the sphere of wisdom. I can possess only a part of the whole, but where two or three believers gather in concord, my access to the meaning of the Bible increases proportionately.

There is an anecdote in the lives of the Desert Fathers that illustrates the necessity of the humility that comes from awareness that alone we do not possess all the truth.

> They tell the story of another old man who persevered in fasting for seventy weeks, eating only once a week. He asked of God about [the meaning of] a certain passage in holy Scripture and God did not reveal it to him. He said to himself, "See how much labor I have undertaken and it has been of no profit to me. I will go, therefore, to my brother and ask him about it." He went outside and closed the door to go out and an angel of the Lord was sent to him, saying, "The seventy weeks you fasted did not make you any closer to God. Now, because you have been humbled and are going off to your brother, I have been sent to explain the passage to you." He opened to him what he sought and then went away.[13]

We may often find that the text of the Bible comes alive in an atmosphere of love, community, and service. Conversely, its meaning is obscured when we allow ourselves to become isolated and concerned only with ourselves. "Religion" cannot, in God's plan, become a substitute for humanity or community.

Our familiarity with the Bible can never become an instrument of personal power over others to proselytize, coerce, judge, or punish them. The Bible has communion as its goal: our being bonded with God and with our fellow humans. We can be sure that we have understood the Bible if it produces love in us and the fruits of the Spirit. It is equally certain that alienation from others, disunity, and a tendency to condemn come from ourselves; they do not derive from God's word.

Despite its intrinsic strength, the word of God comes to us in a very fragile condition: it is unsuitable for battering anyone. The Church Fathers used to speak of the "abbreviated word," *verbum abbreviatum*, a phrase coined on the basis of several texts in the Latin translation of Isaiah.[14] The divine word trimmed itself to our capacities. It did not appear in overwhelming power and splendor but in accessible human form. This was always the manner of God's revelation. It reached its peak in the incarnation, when the second person of the Trinity became subject to space and time and all other human limitations. In so many ancient Christmas sermons, wonderment is expressed that the Word should have become a speechless babe. (It helps to remember that the Latin word *infans* has as its literal meaning "one who does not speak.")[15]

The Scriptures are God's word reduced to a measure of which we are capable. By design the proclamation of the good news is not irresistible. Even the preaching of Jesus did not win for itself an automatic following. What we read in the Bible does not impose itself: its meaning is not always clear nor its persuasiveness automatically effective. Revelation is God's word spoken to our freedom. Its power is not immediately obvious. It must be voluntarily and energetically sought.

The Syrian sixth-century monk who goes under the name Denis the Pseudo-Areopagite speaks of a species of contemplation that is like a corkscrew, mobile with a circular action, endlessly spiralling deeper into God, penetrating to the heart of the divinity. The image signifies that although the contemplative act engages all our energies at each occurrence, it has the potential to increase in intensity as our capacity for love grows. The same is true of our experience of *lectio divina*. Our contact with God is not immediately profound, but reaches profundity only after many years' continuance. Therefore, our initial experience must necessarily be superficial, although at the time we could not realize this. The full benefits of revelation are not accessible to a rapid perusal.

We have to be bold enough to admit that the Bible, despite divine inspiration, is subject to human limitations.[16] It cannot *comprehensively* explain or communicate the reality of God. There is an underlying truth in the Bible's message, but it is a truth expressed on the level of symbol – something that absorbs the attention of our mind and nourishes our spirit but without necessarily providing us with exhaustive information. This is the original meaning of the word "mystery." The Greek term *musterion* is related to the verb *muein* (to contemplate) and means something that has the capacity to sustain prolonged contemplation, something so rich in meaning that the mind readily feeds upon it. We are not talking about a puzzle that, once solved, is left aside. A mystery holds us rapt. Revelation has achieved its goal if it brings us to that total experience of love and understanding that follows our immersion in God.

So profound is the limitation of Scripture that it is a scandal for many – just as the concrete humanity of Jesus scandalized many of his contemporaries (Matthew 11:6). Because the Bible was written between two and three thousand years ago, there is no guarantee that the cultural mind-set it embodies will be acceptable to us. If we believe in the historicity of revelation then we have to accept that the good news about God comes to us embedded in a series of layers of belief that are not of equal importance. Some, such as the assumption of a flat earth and a circulating sun, do not much matter. Other unacceptable elements, although they do not form part of our personal philosophy, need to be retained because they constitute the living skin of revelation – they are not garments that can be discarded. Such themes include the patriarchal bias of biblical cultures, the tendency to discriminate between "elect" and "reprobate" on a racial basis, and the divine sanction of violence and genocide, especially in the functioning of the "ban" (Exodus 23:32f; Deuteronomy 7:1f, 20:16f, Judges 11:30–39; 1 Samuel 15:18f).[17] We cannot leave these aside simply because we do not agree with them – even if we are convinced that they are profoundly wrong. The challenge is for us to find God manifest in these dim and sometimes malignant human constructs. To understand the text we have to put our prejudgments on "hold" and try to enter the mentality of the author, steadfastly refusing to be put off by the incidental idiocies and erroneous opinions that are typical of almost all human beings.[18] The treasure of revelation, like all God's gifts, comes to us in earthen vessels (2 Corinthians 4:7). The wisdom of the Bible is not dependent on clever logic or plausible words; "it is a scandal to the Jews and stupidity to the pagans" (1 Corinthians 1:23). It is only the penetrating eye of the Spirit-filled reader that is able to transcend off-putting first impressions and to find God.

So we need to accept that, even though God's word cuts like a two-edged sword (Hebrews 4:12), it is not God's plan that the Bible be omnipotent. The sowing of the seed produces fruit in proportion to the receptivity of the soil. Revelation is subtle. It does not bludgeon unbelievers into acceptance, but charms the heart of those willing to be wooed. This places a great deal of emphasis on the subjective dispositions of the reader. Three areas in particular may repay our reflection.

First, there is the need for mental preparation. When we read the Bible we cannot presume that its meaning will be immediately apparent to us. Unless we have attained a high competence in scriptural exegesis, we may well find it necessary to prepare for *lectio divina* by some measure of preliminary study. Of this we will speak at great length in a later chapter.

Secondly, there are varying levels of penetration. The repetitive character of *lectio divina* means that we pass through the same territory several times during life. Each time we will find ourselves aware of different aspects of what we are reading. As our perspective changes with experience, we will become more perceptive of the deeper meanings of the text that were previously hidden from us. This means that there is always more richness waiting to be uncovered in the Bible. It also means that as we read, we need to be patient and humble if we do not immediately attain grand insights. Sometimes we have to wander forty years in the desert until our dispositions become such that God's subtle message can penetrate our defenses.

Thirdly, the Spirit comes to the aid of our weakness. When we read with the Church we can be confident that the Holy Spirit is with us, reminding us of the realities of which Scripture speaks and leading us to the fullness of truth. Our reading is not unaided. The Spirit is as active in the reading of the Bible as in its writing, because fundamentally the two activities are complementary facets of a single divine initiative. What good is a communication that is not received? You may write like Shakespeare but it serves no purpose if the letter is not put in the mailbox. In the same way, God not only speaks but also takes steps to ensure that what is spoken is also heard.

To understand the Bible we have to see it in the context of the history of salvation. God entrusts to human beings his word of hope, even knowing that it will become garbled as they pass it from one to another. Many will transmit a message they do not themselves understand or practice, others will exploit it for their own advantage. "Whether dishonestly or in truth, Christ is proclaimed: in this I rejoice" (Philippians 1:18). The seed of the word is sown, a seed that has a mysterious dynamic of growth that those who sow it do not comprehend (Mark 4:27). To all who receive the implanted word in a spirit of meekness, it has the power to bring life (James 1:17). When I read I am opening myself to a God who changes history. I not only receive guidance and comfort, I offer God the opportunity to revolutionize the whole tenor of that segment of history that is my little life.

3

LEVELS OF MEANING

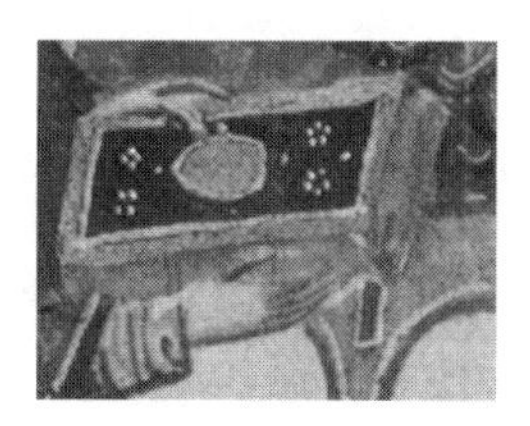

An illustration used by Fulton Sheen in his 1950s television series, *Life Is Worth Living*, remains in my memory. A man jumps off a bridge. Three observers give completely different accounts of the same event. The first is a physicist who speaks about the distance, speed, acceleration, duration, and impact of the fall from bridge to water. The second is a psychologist who discusses it in terms of inner drives, unconscious processes, and motivation. The third is a priest who views what happened through the prism of ethics and theology. The point Bishop Sheen made was that it is possible to give different accounts of a single incident; each presents the facts in its own way. The image reminds us that whenever we human beings attempt to speak the truth, we envisage only one aspect of the reality and so the result is necessarily partial.

So much depends on the strength of our sensibilities. To walk through a rainforest with one who knows and loves the area is far superior to being with mere tourists looking for photo opportunities. One who loves sees more, because love is also a way of access to the truth.[1] As we grow in love we gain a richer understanding of the object of our affection. There are other ways also in which our understanding is deepened: by knowledge, by personal growth, by being with enthusiasts, by cherishing a wider experience of reality. The same spot can look so different when I am in a different space. Human beings in a state of health are constantly changing and, as a result, our experience of life is not the same from one year to the next.

This is an important truth to bear in mind when it comes to reflecting on our practice of *lectio divina*. Sacred reading speaks to my present situation. Another way of expressing this is to say: I perceive the message of Scripture partially according to my present sensitivity.[2] The more quiet and unhindered my mind and heart, the wider my horizons. If I am being tossed around by anger, envy, or lust or weighed down by grief and emptiness, it is likely that God's word will address a narrower spectrum of concern. What a beginner perceives in Scripture may be more dramatic but less profound than what is experienced by veterans with a lifetime's fidelity behind them. Abba Nesteros, one of the Desert Fathers whose words were collected by John Cassian, speaks of this reality:

> As our mind is increasingly renewed by this study [of the Scriptures], the face of the Scriptures also begins to be renewed. It is as though the beauty of a more sacred understanding keeps pace with our progress. The Scriptures accommodate themselves to the capacity of human perception; what appears to be earthly to the carnal seems divine to the spiritual.[3]

Like the manna collected by Israel in the desert, there is only enough spiritual nourishment for one day. We cannot store it to save ourselves future exertion. "If *today* you hear God's voice, harden not your heart" (Psalm 95:7–8). True, some of us can, like camels, live off our humps for a while – but the supply is not inexhaustible and it depends on our having previously absorbed substantial intake. Most people's experience is that it is necessary to keep a thread of continuity in their exposure to Scripture. That way God's word does not become stale; renewed frequently, it adapts to our changing life. Instead of being an exercise for routine's sake it becomes a vital component of our desire to live our lives in the context of the divine.

What we see in God's word changes both qualitatively and as a matter of degree. There is no reason for our *lectio divina* to be completely homogeneous. This will lead to boredom and eventual estrangement from the Scriptures. It is helpful to know that there are different facets of the biblical texts that can serve us in distinctive ways in our efforts to understand what God has revealed to us and take action. The different truths to be found in the Scriptures were described by the Church Fathers as the "senses" of Scriptures. It may be helpful for us to reflect on this theme.

The "four senses" of Scripture

The ancient expositors of the Bible were conscious that its words were full of mystery. By their own experience they knew that there was a power in the inspired word that transcended the overt purpose or meaning of a particular text. How often the reading of Scripture becomes the occasion of a major illumination or conversion. Whereas many modern exegetes are reluctant to see more in the Bible than its historico-critical meaning, tradition has long accepted the possibility of a *sensus plenior*, a "fuller sense," that discloses itself to the faith-filled reader.

It is not that specialists in the Bible object to Scripture being stretched in homiletics or devotion. There is no doubt that Scripture is an evocative medium and that its persuasiveness can be enhanced by inserting a text in a different setting. The point they are making is that such added meanings are extrinsic to the inspired word. They are not implicit in the text itself, hidden there by the divine author and dependent on human industry for their uncovering. Despite what many of the Church Fathers averred, the account of Abraham's encounter with God at the Oak of Mamre (Genesis 18) does *not* contain "foreshadowings" of the doctrine of the Holy Trinity.[4] The exegetes are not necessarily attempting to quench such poetic extensions, but merely to say that they are not a necessary element for an authentic understanding of the text.

Such reserve defines the frontiers of the "fuller sense." These parameters are important for those who deal with the Bible professionally. For those of us who read the Scriptures mainly for personal profit, we can afford to be a little more free. The more-than-literal meanings of the Bible can often help us to absorb, retain, and express what the Scriptures proclaim. A poor photograph or a bad recording does not convey the vitality of the original, yet it may help us to come closer to what is represented and to retain it more fully in awareness. In the same way, even extravagant literary excursions can sometimes help us to become more involved in the biblical text with the result that it has greater power to influence us.[5]

The revealing work of the Holy Spirit did not cease with the drying of the ink on the last page of the Book of Revelation. Inspiration, properly speaking, is the guidance given to that complex of activities that resulted in the *writing* of the biblical books.[6] The Spirit is also active, however, in the *reading* of Scripture. If the Bible is a place of encounter with God, both for the person and for the community, then it is clear these extra meanings are not arbitrary impressions; they also are probably prompted by the Spirit. Yes, they are subject to discernment. No, we cannot guarantee that every private "inspiration" is a direct message from God. We simply affirm that for one who is seeking God in a spirit of openness to the future, and with an ample supply of both common sense and integrity, occasions of going badly astray are relatively few. We are not infallible and sometimes we misread persons, situations, and texts; no great harm is done if we have an ordinary level of prudence and humility. Conversely, if we are too scrupulous in our reading, fearful of making mistakes, we may limit our horizons excessively and miss some of the potential fruits of *lectio divina*.

The possibility of alternative senses in the Bible is the foundation of sacred reading. Study gives us the objective meaning of the text, but there are other processes that facilitate a more holistic response to God's word. *Lectio* and study are not to be identified, though they may sometimes overlap. We will return to this point later. For the moment it is necessary only to envisage *lectio divina* as that dealing with the text that begins where study leaves off. This is where the traditional teaching about the multiple "senses" of Scripture is useful.

As one might expect with such an unwieldy body of literature, there is a certain amount of disagreement among the various Fathers about how many senses of Scripture exist and what they are. For those interested, a French Jesuit has published an 1,800-page study of the subject.[7] Although as many as seven levels of meaning were distinguished, most preferred three or four.

The literal sense. This is sometimes called the historical meaning. It is what the author consciously intended to communicate in writing, whether it be a story, a doctrine, or a moral exhortation. This is the meaning of Scripture that is accessible to professional biblical scholarship. Most of the Fathers agree that until this level is adequately mastered, there is no point in progressing to the other levels. Abandoning the literal meaning will likely lead to error.

The christological sense. The so-called "allegorical sense" is an attempt to find added Christian meaning in otherwise arid passages of Scripture. This involved relocating any particular text within the context of the totality of salvation. It is a little like reading a murder mystery knowing the identity of the murderer. The significance of many little incidents becomes clear to us. In the same way, Christians read the Old Testament knowing what the final outcome will be. And this is not only abstract knowledge; believers are in experiential contact with the order of grace. When, for instance, they read in Genesis the story of the Fall, they tend to interpret it in terms of the "happy fault" about which the Easter liturgy sings. In the same way, when Saint Augustine explains the Psalms, he often relies on the letters of Saint Paul – not so much to explain the words as to appreciate the permanent realities to which the words give expression.

Recourse to the allegorical sense was a means of building up faith. The conclusions were often sound, although the ways of reaching them seem bizarre to us.[8] Unless we move easily in the sphere of poetic license, it is probable that we will feel uncomfortable with some of the traditional examples of arriving at the Christological sense. On the other hand, it seems to me unnatural to expect a fervent Christian to read of God's promises and not to think immediately of their realization in the historical Jesus, in the present reality of grace and the working of the Holy Spirit, and in the future hope of eternal life. To understand the God who made promises to Abraham and Sarah, it helps to superimpose our Christian experience of grace on the ancient narratives – as we find in Romans 4 and Hebrews 11. The Christological meaning is what emerges when a text is read in a fuller awareness of the spiritual realities about which the text is speaking.

The behavioral sense. This is also called the "moral" or "tropological" sense. This terminology does not refer to the objective ethical content of Scripture, but to the way in which God's word shapes our beliefs and values so as eventually to evangelize our behavior. It was this sense that the monastic authors favored. The Scriptures are given to form our behavior, to make us Christlike. Whatever they impart by way of information – including theological information – is secondary to their role in the practical reformation of daily life according to the teaching and example of Jesus. "Blessed are those who hear God's word – and keep it" (Luke 11:28). As Saint James reminds us, we are called to be "doers of the word and not hearers only" (James 1:22–25).

The mystical sense. The technical term for this was the "anagogical" sense, referring to the Bible's power to lift up hearts to spiritual realities and to make us feel a greater desire for the things of God, to lead us ever deeper into prayer. This is the component of the Good News that is constantly calling us into communion – with God and with our neighbor. As we read we become more aware of an attraction within to transcend the pettiness that characterizes so much of our lives and to open ourselves more fully to God present in the sacrament of the word. To allow desire for God to become paramount in our lives, to "abide" in God and to allow God to abide in us. The Gospel of John, especially, invites a reading that operates at this level.

To some extent the four senses are sequential. This can be a helpful way of approaching *lectio divina*, so long as we remember that there is a lot of backing and forthing as well as overlaps between the stages. We begin with a diligent attention to the literal meaning of the text. We allow our reading to contextualize itself within the totality of salvation so that, unbidden, every page of the Scriptures sings to us of Christ. The confidence that our faith inspires gives us courage to look at the reality of daily life and to imprint on it a genuine evangelical character. The struggles involved in this and the inevitable failures lead us to recognize our limits and so we call out to God for help. Out of our experience of weakness prayer is born.[9] As God responds to our prayer we begin to have some experience of what God is like. As familiarity increases our appreciation of God grows, and with it spiritual desire and a secret yearning for communion with God. When this union occurs, as it does sometimes, we begin to understand why the ancients regarded *lectio divina* as a school of contemplation.

The same process could be described in terms of the faculties activated in the different moments of our relationship with the inspired text. In our industrious uncovering of the literal meaning of a text, we employ our senses (obviously) and our *intellect*. This is the level of brain work, where correct conclusions do not necessarily depend on faith or commitment. The Christological sense operates in a different space. It engages our *memory*. What we read is gradually relocated in an existing world of meaning, touched by grace and with a high level of personal persuasiveness. Progressively our *conscience* is activated. The word now comes to us as an inner command, understood only in honesty and embraced only by a practical willingness to obey.[10] More and more, *lectio divina* is being marked by a relational character. We are more truthfully conscious both of God and of our essential selves. At this point the word has penetrated to the inmost level of our being, to the summit of our personhood. The word is addressed to our *spirit*, and at that level we become aware that the Word is no longer an intermediary between us and God; we experience the Word as Person.

In the next section we will look at another way of distinguishing the different moments within the complex process of *lectio divina*. What begins as reading becomes reflection or meditation; this leads to prayer and ultimately to contemplative union with God. The Latin terms used traditionally are *lectio* > *meditatio* > *oratio* > *contemplatio*. Before passing to examine this aspect of sacred reading, however, it may be useful to give a diagram that summarizes schematically what we have been saying.

The Four Moments of *Lectio Divina*

	SENSE	FACULTY	FUNCTION	PRAYER
1.	Literal	Intellect	Understanding the text	*Lectio*
2.	Christological	Memory	Contextualizing the meaning	*Meditatio*
3.	Behavioral	Conscience	Living the meaning	*Oratio*
4.	Mystical	Spirit	Meeting God in the text	*Contemplatio*

As with every schema there is a degree of oversimplification in this. The potential advantage in reducing such a complex matter to its elements is that it gives a checklist to see whether there is something lacking to the integrity of *lectio divina* in our practice. Sacred reading will function creatively over a lifetime only if it is allowed to fulfill, at one point or another, all the functions that this diagram suggests.

From reading to prayer

The classic delineation of the four moments of prayer associated with *lectio divina* is to be found in a late twelfth century treatise known under the title *The Ladder of Monastics* (*Scala Claustralium*). This is a letter on the contemplative life written by Guigo II, the ninth Prior of the Grand Chartreuse.[11] It is a short work (the English translation comprises less than twenty normal pages) and it is not difficult to read. The content is typical of the best of Latin monastic spirituality of the time.

The idea of a ladder was very important to monastic authors. Saint John Climacus (Greek *klimax* = ladder) wrote a whole book about spiritual ladders. Likewise, the most important part of Saint Benedict's Rule is his long chapter on the ladder of humility.[12] A ladder is a means of ascending from one level to another. Monastic writers used the image to give an account of the different stages of the ascent to God. Some wrote prescriptively: this is what you must do to keep going higher. Others, like Saint Benedict, wrote descriptively: this is what you will experience as grace draws you upwards toward God. Ladders were important because they were a way of dealing with the dynamic and changeable aspects of the spiritual life – and this in a world that had no word for "development" or "evolution" and in which reality was regarded as fundamentally static and the earth was flat. Ladders are the response of experience to philosophy. Rational thought may have assumed universal unchanging laws, but experience knew that in human affairs substantial changes occur as life progresses.

Guigo aims to describe how it is possible for us to experience contemplative communion with God. The system he expounds is one developed over the centuries as a result of experience. It is not simply a theoretical construct. It makes no claim to being the only way to God. Guigo simply sets forth in greater detail how it has come about that many monks have found contemplation.

The worst thing we could possibly do is to regard the treatise as a recipe book and attempt to cook up some contemplation for ourselves. The "system" Guigo expounds is not rigid and prescriptive. Its stages are more like the colors of a rainbow than bureaucratic categories. The different moments ebb and flow; sometimes they overlap, at others they drift apart. In the various seasons of our life we can expect different blends of elements: at one stage more reading, at another absorption in quiet satisfies all our spiritual hunger.

Above all, the four steps that Guigo envisages – reading, meditation, prayer, contemplation – do not constitute a "method" of prayer to be implemented mechanically in one session. Sometimes the steps of the ladder are not chronologically connected. The prayer latent in meditation on Scripture is released unpredictably later when engaged in an entirely different activity. Some people combine reading, reflection, and prayer in a single "exercise"; others separate them in time and space. Many experience a delayed reaction. The impact of their *lectio* may strike months later. There is a lot of flexibility here that takes seriously different characters, different vocations, different opportunities, and the changing seasons of life.

Contemplation can never be seen as the outcome of a process. It remains a gift from God that is not automatically associated with particular human acts. It is given in God's time not as a "reward" for work well done, but as an energizing component within the total context of life. This means that the earlier stages of the process attempt to increase our receptivity; their outcome will depend on what we are and the reality of our life. For some people the conditions will obtain quickly; in others it takes a lifetime of struggle and confusion to arrive at the point of being willing to accept what God desires to give.

Guigo begins his treatment by emphasizing the distance between the beginnings and the end. Like Jacob's ladder (Genesis 28:12), the foot rests on lowly earth, whereas the top penetrates the hidden heights of heaven.

> One day I was engaged in physical work with my hands and I began to think about the spiritual tasks we humans have. While I was thinking, four spiritual steps came to mind, namely, reading, meditation, prayer, and contemplation. This is the ladder of monastics by which they are lifted up from earth into heaven. There are only a few distinct steps, but the distance covered is beyond measure and belief since the lower part is fixed on the earth and its top passes through the clouds to lay bare the secrets of heaven.[13]

What we have here is something that counters the charge of elitism that is sometimes leveled against those who promote Christian contemplation. Yes, contemplation is a high human activity, and it is true that at this moment not all are capable of it. The encouraging and optimistic conviction that Guigo embodies is that it is possible for us to ascend to what is higher. If we have a passion for the higher gifts (1 Corinthians 12:31), then a means of making an advance in that direction is here laid out before us.

Guigo affirms that simple dedication to God's word, if carried to its logical conclusion, will conduct us to the lofty zones of contemplative intimacy with God. Thus it can be said that the ultimate goal of *lectio divina* is contemplation. And according to the ancient way of viewing reality, the final aim of any project must stamp itself on each of the preliminary steps if any progress is to be made. In other words, although there are different moments in the process of sacred reading, they all need to have a prayer-like character.

Although properly speaking there is question of a unitary process, it can be helpful to distinguish the different moments that mark the gradual transition from the active task of reading to the graced state of absorption in God. In this way we can cooperate more responsibly when we become aware of being drawn deeper and deeper into mystery. This is Guigo's summary of his teaching:

> So that you can better see the totality of what has been spoken of in separate sections, let us put together a summary that recapitulates what has already been said. You can see by the examples already proposed how the steps belong together and how some precede others both in time and in causation. Reading is like a first foundation; it gives us matter for meditation. Meditation seeks more diligently what is to be sought. It is like the digging that finds a treasure (Proverbs 2:4, Matthew 13:44) and brings it to light. However, of itself it is unable to gain possession of the treasure, and so we are led to prayer. Prayer raises itself up with all its might towards God and pleads for the desirable treasure that is the sweetness of contemplation. With the advent of contemplation comes the reward of all these previous labors. The thirsting soul is inebriated by the dew of heavenly sweetness. Reading is an exterior exercise; meditation belongs to the interior intellect. Prayer operates at the level of desire. Contemplation

> transcends every sense. Reading is proper to beginners, meditation to proficients, prayer to those with devotion and contemplation to the blessed.[14]

Fundamentally it is the atmosphere of prayer that penetrates every aspect of holy reading that makes it distinctive. Prayer is not suddenly born at the third stage. Rather, prayer accompanies us as we open the book and settle our mind, as we read the page and ponder its meaning. Prayer is the meaning of *lectio divina*; that is why the exercise of sacred reading is sometimes said to be a technique of prayer.

When prayer comes naturally or with only a little coaxing, everything is fine. We don't need to examine our practice or read books about *lectio divina*. It is almost a case of sitting back and letting prayer take over. At other times, however, the situation is a little more difficult. Perhaps we are emotionally or intellectually stimulated or restless or depressed. We begin to read but somehow get sidetracked. We might be like the monks of whom Guerric of Igny speaks:

> Now they are present at the divine praises and fall asleep or occupy themselves with idle and pernicious thoughts. They sit down with a book but yawn. They hear a word of exhortation, but it is hard work for them to listen.[15]

How do we cope with a situation like that? The general rule is simple; if prayer is not found then insert it. Begin the reading with a prayer, interrupt the text with prayer. Some people find it useful to translate each verse that they read into an address to God that springs from the reality of their own life and experience. Most often, if we tackle a text in this way and demonstrate our seriousness, the impermeable façade will crack and spontaneous prayer will begin to tumble from the text. This is because the apparent prayerlessness of a text is more often really a matter of our subjective dispositions. When we get in touch with our desire to pray and leave aside the obtrusive inner resistances that block our endeavor, things go better.

Prayerful reading is the first moment of *lectio divina*. Everything that facilitates prayer will contribute something positive to our reading of the Scriptures. However, by making explicit at the very beginning of our perusal of the text our desire to meet God, we are already opening the way to a deeper understanding. The best answer to the question, "Why am I doing this?" is "I hope to find God in my reading." *Lectio divina* is an expression of my search for God. Sacred reading can be considered "successful" only if it causes me to drop my defenses and allow God to touch my heart and change my life. To activate my latent faith and confidence in God by an act of will is an ideal way to start. Ironically, the worse I feel myself to be at the beginning, the more likely it is that I will open myself to God's gracious intervention.

Some practical directives to foster such a disposition will be found in the next chapter. For the moment it is sufficient to insist again that prayer does not wait for the third stage of the process. In some sense it needs to be present from the outset. This is chiefly what distinguishes *lectio divina* from study, recreation, and other forms of reading. It would be a mistake to think that Guigo envisages a prayerless reading as his first step. The stages are distinguished, but they are not to be separated, much less to be considered potentially autonomous.

> From what has been said we may gather that reading without meditation is dry. Meditation without reading is subject to error. Prayer without meditation is lukewarm. Meditation without prayer is fruitless. Prayer with devotion leads to contemplation whereas contemplation without prayer happens rarely or by a miracle.[16]

To revert to his image of the ladder, Guigo affirms that in normal circumstances we need to have climbed the lower rungs before attempting the ones at the top. At the same time, the purpose of the ascent remains identical throughout the entire process. We climb a ladder to reach the top. Our desire for the summit of contemplation is what drives us all through the climb, even though, at the moment, our energies are concentrated on the lower levels. We are forced first to work at lowlier tasks that are closer to the reality of our lives.

The first task is to ensure that the process begins on the right track. This means that we make time to open the Bible and read it. We are also obliged to do everything possible to ensure that our reading of the text is objective and accurate. The fundamental necessity of diligence in seeking the literal sense of Scripture will be discussed in the next section.

Finding the literal sense

Lectio divina leads to a conscious endeavor to live in accordance with the Gospels. To live what we read. Because evangelical living grows from what we understand of the Gospels, it is important to ensure that we are really grasping what God has revealed in the Scriptures. Otherwise, we may reduce the awesome word of God to our own imaginary constructions. Berno of Reichenau, an eleventh-century monk, was aware of this possibility. "Prudent reader, always beware of a superstitious understanding. Do not try to accommodate the Scriptures to your own meanings or add your own meanings to the Scriptures."[17]

It is certainly true that our sacred reading takes place under the guidance of the Holy Spirit and, in general, of God's Providence. This, however, is no excuse for failing to exercise normal human industry and prudence in arriving at an interpretation that corresponds to the intrinsic meaning of the text. One of the strongest deterrents to long-term fidelity to *lectio divina* is a sort of pious laziness that does not permit the mind to become actively engaged. There is an attitude abroad that is suspicious of study and intellectual effort. I am often surprised to hear well-educated preachers propound an interpretation of the Gospel text that owes nothing to biblical research. Underlying their exposition is the assumption that the meaning of Scripture is plain and no more than common sense is required to understand what is written. Languages and the skills of biblical interpretation are too easily dismissed as irrelevant to preaching or to practical discipleship. Instead, the sacred text is often approached in a state of mental disengagement that would be judged unacceptable in most other spheres of human activity.

In one sense there is not much point in spending time with the Scriptures if we are not diligent in searching out the authentic meaning of the text before us. The Bible is not an easy book to read. It is an anthology of texts from distant cultures written two to three thousand years ago. It seems to me that we will never understand the Bible unless we appreciate just how alien it is. The ancient monks were certainly aware of this and took great pains to consult whatever authorities were available that might unlock the authentic meaning of the inspired word. Saint Stephen Harding, one of the Cistercian founders, was so zealous in this matter that he published his own revision of the Latin Bible, consulting the rabbis wherever the Hebrew text was obscure – rather an extraordinary openness in twelfth-century Europe.

It is true that there are passages in the Scriptures that speak to us with urgency and passion even without preparation on our part. It is also true that we often fumble and miss the meaning of a text simply because we have not taken the trouble to do the necessary spade work. I am often reminded of something Saint Thérèse of Lisieux said two months before she died:

> Had I been a priest, I would have learned Hebrew and Greek, and wouldn't have been satisfied with Latin. In this way I would have known the real text dictated by the Holy Spirit.[18]

Love for the Scriptures makes us want to be sure that it is really God's word that we receive and not merely feedback from our own opinions and prejudgments.

I am suggesting that in many cases, before we begin spending a lot of time on a particular book of the Bible, it can be useful to spend some time in preparatory study. Before we begin a journey it makes sense to consult a map and acquire a basic familiarity with the major routes, even though the details may be left open. We may also profit from a tourist guide that will alert us to what is noteworthy in the area and give us information that will help us to appreciate what we see. In the same way, the adventure of taking up a new segment of the Bible can be enhanced by our having some general knowledge about the book and its contents.

Access to the information we need will vary from person to person. Some feel comfortable signing on for courses at theological schools, others prefer a non-academic program or participation in a study group. For those with such opportunities, guidelines for reading will be given. Here I would like to give some general indications for those who are working away quietly on their own. At the risk of discouraging a potential reader, I would like to list all the areas in which information can be helpful to an accurate reading of the inspired text, although I recognize that most of us are able to pursue only one line of inquiry at a time.

Background culture. Many narratives in the Old Testament and even the parables of Jesus make sense only if we have some knowledge of the customs of the time. What is a covenant? How much was a talent or denarius worth? Who were the Zealots or the Pharisees? What was the etiquette at a wedding feast? What is "the abomination of desolation"? In what precise sense was the word *Abba* used? These and a thousand other simple questions occur to us as we read. Finding answers to them will often lead us to a richer understanding of the meaning of the sacred text. Some annotated Bibles and many single-volume commentaries contain articles on biblical background and culture. For specific points, some of the readily-available biblical dictionaries will provide us with the information we need.[19]

Biblical languages. Of course, not all of us will have the opportunity to learn Hebrew and Greek, but those who have should make the most of it. If we are not so lucky, at least we can learn a little about the idiom of the Bible, because there are some words and phrases which have a special meaning that does not always translate easily into modern languages. If we have access to a theological library there are giant volumes there that will provide ten times as much information as we need.[20] On the other hand, William Barclay's *New Testament Words* gives a clear picture of the broader context of many significant New Testament expressions in terms any interested person can understand.[21]

Methods of composition. The books of the Bible were not written in the same way as modern works. They are not so much individual compositions as monuments to the corporate memory. Few of the books of the Bible derive from a single author. Many of them contain material from different sources, reflecting different concerns and viewpoints. Sometimes the material began as an oral tradition and was written down a long time later. In nearly all cases the resulting book belongs more to the group in which it originated than to any individual – including the one whose name it may bear. Each book is different and it is helpful to read a good introduction that will give us a thread to follow through the labyrinth. Many passages that seem contradictory become clearer when we are able to identify the different elements that have been lumped together to form the whole. A good example is found in the Bible's opening pages. There are two distinct accounts of creation, with some elements in common but many differences. To appreciate the particular viewpoints of both accounts helps us to understand the profundity of the mystery of creation. The divergence in the two stories ceases to be a difficulty; it is recognized as an enrichment.

Literary genres. Following from the former point, our understanding of the biblical text will be enhanced by an appreciation of "literary genres." This is to say that we need to know what sort of writing is before us: whether it be history or imaginative fiction, doctrinal statement or pastoral exhortation. We also need to realize that some of the forms used in antiquity are unfamiliar to modern readers. The Second Vatican Council insisted that interpreters pay attention to literary genres:

> Since in sacred Scripture, God speaks to us through human beings and in human fashion, the interpreter of the sacred Scriptures, if he or she is to perceive what God has wished to communicate to us, should carefully investigate the meaning which the sacred authors really had in mind and which it pleased God to manifest through their words.
>
> To find the intention of the sacred writers, attention must be paid, among other things, to literary forms. For the truth is presented in a variety of ways and expressed variously in historical writing, prophetic and poetic texts and in other forms of speech. Hence the exegete must pursue the meaning that the sacred writer, in a particular situation and in special circumstances of time and culture, intended and expressed, through the medium of a contemporary literary form. To understand correctly what the sacred author intended to affirm, due attention must be paid both to the usual and accepted patterns of perception, speech and narrative that were in use at the time of the sacred writer and the conventions that people of this time followed in their interaction.[22]

It is true that this recommendation is directed specifically to professional exegetes, but the same consideration holds for us all. Any trouble we go to in order to safeguard the integrity of the Bible's meaning is a sure sign that we are sincere in our desire to place God's word at the center of our lives.

Cross referencing. It is often very enlightening to interpret the Bible through the Bible – to read texts in the light of similar passages. For this, a good memory is helpful or, failing that, a concordance of the Bible. A concordance gives us reference to all the occurrences of a particular word and so we are able to look up other texts that relate to what we are reading. A little caution is needed, however, since concordances are based on a particular translation. If we are using a different version of Scripture, a little imagination will be necessary to find the equivalent word. The commonest and most economical concordance is Cruden's, begun in the eighteenth century and based on the King James Bible. A browse in the bookshops will unearth others.[23]

Theological synthesis. There are scores of books available on "biblical theology," though not of equal value. Almost any of them, however, can alert us to the broader significance of particular themes and help us to bring to the text we are reading a mind that is attuned to the totality of revelation. Everything we read has its own spot in history; to appreciate its history and to know where it is leading will help us to be sensitive to the authentic message that this particular text carries.[24]

Skills of interpretation. The art of exegesis (or explanation of the biblical text) involves putting together data from all the above sources and being able to give a solid opinion about the meaning of the text. It is not afraid to use words like "possibly" or "probably," and it is always open to change as new data arrives on the scene. Professional exegetes have to be very industrious in weighing not only facts but also the opinions of their peers. We who read for personal profit can often be content with a more general awareness of the issues. There is a danger that with limited time and energy we may postpone forever any certainty about finding the literal sense of the Bible and, as a result, never continue the work by applying it to our own lives. Each one of us, therefore, according to the possibilities of our own situation, needs to work out what proportion of our time is to be given to study and what left for prayerful, life-oriented reflection.

If it happens that we have time to read a verse-by-verse commentary on a particular book, there are two principal alternatives.

First there are single-volume commentaries that encompass the whole Bible.[25] Usually the contributors are recognized specialists in their field and the authors of larger works. All the major issues are raised and brief answers are given to most questions. Inevitably, however, the more extensive the coverage, the less profound the treatment of individual points. It is convenient to have a reference volume for the whole Bible, but often the explanation of a particular text is not detailed enough to provide the sort of stimulus we seek. The same implicit criticism can be levelled at "introductions" to the Bible. Information is too thinly spread to have much impact. If we only want to know about one or two books, we would gain more from having recourse to the appropriate specialized treatments.

On the other hand, if a particular book interests us we can try to find a good commentary – one that is written by an expert and will be read by scholars, but which is also comprehensible to a non-specialist. Many scriptural monographs and commentaries produced in the last decades (particularly by American publishers) qualify. Raymond Brown's two-volume commentary on John is an excellent preparation for *lectio divina.*[26] Someone who teaches Scripture or a well-informed bookseller can often point us towards titles that will serve our purpose.[27] No one need be surprised that there will be parts of these books that we must blithely ignore: the foreign footnotes, the clash of scholarly opinion, and the interminable discussions on points of grammar. We may need to hiccup as we come to Greek and Hebrew words – even though most authors nowadays give English equivalents and don't presume that we know what they are talking about. Yes, a little forbearance is necessary, but if we persevere we will often find that our understanding is expanded so that when finally we come to reading the biblical book in a climate of prayer, we reap the fruit of our labors. The more educated we are in our own field of specialization, the more necessary it is to reach a comparable level of intelligence with regard to the Scriptures. If we have a high level of expertise in our own profession, it is unlikely that primary-school information on the Bible will be sufficient to engage our intelligence.

What this means is that serious, lifelong readers of the Bible will probably feel drawn gradually to acquire half a dozen books or more to help them understand it better.[28] These volumes need to do more than merely decorate the wall; they should be used often enough for them to become familiar. The easier it is for us to find our way around their contents, the more likely it is that we will consult them when we have a question. When it comes to tools of the trade, the professional will need to keep up with the latest trends. For those of us whose exegesis is more of the do-it-yourself variety, our first set of reference volumes may well last a lifetime. The fact that they are not quite state-of-the-art is balanced by ease of use from long familiarity.

Instead of a shelf of books we may prefer to use an annotated Bible. This will provide us with a great deal of additional information as we read. Any of the following annotated Bibles will contribute to a better understanding of the biblical text.

The HarperCollins Study Bible was produced by the Society of Biblical Literature and is based on the New Revised Standard Version. It has about 2,400 pages with introductions, maps, and chronological tables as well as substantial textual notes.

The New Oxford Annotated Bible with Apocrypha was edited by Bruce M. Metzger and Roland E. Murphy and published by Oxford University Press. It is based on the NRSV translation and provides a similar body of information to the previous title, but is a little more expensive. Earlier editions of this Bible remain useful.

The New Jerusalem Bible is both translation and provider of information. This is a revision of the original 1966 edition. Similar in scope to the previous works, it makes available in English the advances in scholarship represented by the 1973 edition of the *Bible de Jérusalem*. Earlier editions of this Bible remain useful.

Sometimes it is helpful during this preliminary study to compare two translations. If we are really keen, it is possible to acquire a parallel Bible which gives four of the most modern translations side by side on the page for instant comparison.[29] In this way we can glean some idea of the range of possible meanings for any text without having to shuffle books and pages. It is useful for study purposes, but probably not so good for *lectio divina*.

Apart from making use of these standard aids we can sometimes employ other methods to establish a general familiarity with what we are reading. Some people read through a book quickly and then go back to the beginning and recommence in a slower, *lectio* mode. Sometimes instructors can plot "walking paths" through a particular book. Like pathways through a national park, these enable us to traverse much of the ground and see a representative sample of the environment, without attempting total coverage. These "paths" can be based on themes or events or literary characteristics. After having read through these criss-crossing references, we would become reasonably familiar with the style and content of the book. When we began to use it for *lectio*, we would probably have little difficulty in gauging the original meaning and context of a particular passage. The preliminary work of familiarization bears fruit in a more intelligent reading of the text in its entirety and probably in a heightened sense of devotion.

In this section we have been talking about strategies that will help us understand the biblical text more fully and accurately. Such tactics will succeed to the extent that they bring us to a better contact with the Scriptures. If using the various instruments becomes a distraction that leads us away from a personal reading of the text, then obviously they are not serving their purpose as *preparation* for sacred reading. Study in order to find the literal sense of the Bible is useful in its own right, but its value is enhanced when it is subordinated to a person-to-person encounter with God's word. It is in facilitating such contact that preliminary study has much to offer – even for those who do not consider themselves natural students.

Mindfulness

Our sacred reading is conditioned by what we bring to it – our personal salvation history, our recent experience, our overt faith and obedience. In the previous section we have seen how some preliminary study can be helpful.

All these elements go into the blender, and when we push the button to start, they are what determines the quality of the final product. At the other end of *lectio* there is also cause and effect. The fruitfulness of sacred reading depends not only on what contributes to the process or what happens while the book is open. Much hinges on what we do with what we receive. The seed of the word yields the most plentiful harvest when it continues to be nurtured patiently in welcoming soil. In the traditional understanding of the process it is the memory that acts as the receiver of the word and the instrument by which the gospel is able to exercise an influence on behavior.[30]

God's word incarnates itself in our lives as an element of dialogue. It is an initiative that begs for an answer, and it is only in responding that we demonstrate that our hearts have welcomed the contact. There is no guarantee that we will immediately grasp the significance of what is said to us, especially if there is a question of a message that challenges our habitual perceptions. Like a difficult book that we really want to master, God's word often demands perseverance of us. We have to stay with it while we adjust to a different perspective and not lightly dismiss the relevance of what exceeds our present understanding. Instead, let us give God's word entry into our memory to give ourselves the chance to become less fearful of its unaccustomed rigor and more appreciative of its potential to lead us to life.

Memory is the bridge between hearing the word and putting it into practice. This is clear from so many texts in the book of Deuteronomy.[31] The key to present vitality is mindfulness of the past. Active efforts to keep the memory of God's word alive (6:1–9, 11:18–28) permit us to be alert and learn from experience (4:9–10). Since lack of freedom is often a matter of being unable to distance ourselves from immediate influence, it follows that any schooling in a broader perspective will be liberating (4:39–40). If we remember the lessons learned in hard times, we can avoid the necessity of repeating the experience (8:1–6). If we are mindful of our history, which includes both our liabilities (9:6–8) and our assets (14:1–2), then the past prompts us to fair dealing in the present. The word remains present to us and leads us to free, adult choice (30:1–5, 11–20). Instead of submitting to fate, we can thus make our own selection between blessing and curse (28:9–11, 15, 47–48).

Memory is less cultivated in education now than in the earlier part of this century. As a result, our perception of the present often lacks depth. One who does not learn from the mistakes of history is doomed to repeat them. Yet memory (or tradition) is assailed from both left and right. The left attacks it because the past is identified with the forces of conservatism; it is understood, to use Margaret Mead's terms, as "coercive" rather than "instrumental."[32] It imposes its own way of viewing situations and responding to them so that development is blocked. On the other hand, memory is rejected by the right because it is subversive to the *status quo*; memory knows another time. It relativizes the present and so can offer an alternative to current ideology – which may be why J. B. Metz speaks about "the dangerous memory of Jesus Christ."[33]

If we are to speak about the memory as one of the means that can facilitate our responsiveness to spiritual growth, then we can probably expect a certain degree of unconscious opposition to the proposal. Memory is more than the ability to recall information. In the traditional sense it involves living in the presence of what is "remembered," just as mindfulness of a loved one may accompany all our activities. This is what Jesus meant when he spoke about "abiding" or "remaining" in his word (John 8:31; 15:7).[34] To live in the presence of God alters our behavior and also effects a qualitative change in our experience. It is a dynamic element in ongoing conversion. Perhaps this is why we resist it. Many wise persons from the time of Deuteronomy have thought "forgetfulness" and, in particular, forgetfulness of God is the fundamental aberration of the human spirit.[35] And the way back to God, as illustrated in the parable of the Prodigal Son (Luke 15:11–32), begins when we remember who we are and how much our Father loves us.

Our sacred reading is not merely for the moment. We read with the purpose of evangelizing our lives – just as we eat not only to enjoy the taste of food but to nourish our whole body and generate sufficient energy to implement our ambitions. If *lectio divina* has no effect beyond the few moments of its exercise, then it is scarcely worth doing. It has been reduced to the level of devotional self-indulgence.

This is easy to understand in theory. As usual, practice is trickier. Why, I ask myself, do I not remember more of what I read? Why do I not let God's word flow more freely into my life? It seems to me that there are several overlapping reasons.

Inattention. If our sacred reading is irregular and perfunctory it is unlikely that the words will build up sufficient clout to shake our habitual complacency. We get into the habit of paying minimal attention to what we read. In this chapter we have been discussing different levels of meaning. If we do not go beyond the superficial, then it may happen that there is no meeting point between the text and what is currently occurring in our lives. As a result the Bible remains merely a matter of words. We read texts, they saunter nonchalantly across the surface of our mind and fall off the edge never to be heard of again. Unless we stop them and engage in dialogue with them, even the holiest passages of Scripture will leave us unmoved and unchanged. In the next chapter we will talk about practical ways of becoming involved with what we read.

Hardheartedness. The word of God will never be active in our memory if it is ignored through inattention. The same outcome follows when we manifest such a defensive attitude that nothing can penetrate the hardened husk of a heart unwilling to be corrected. What does not enter will never be retained; what is not retained can never be recalled. The admonition of Psalm 95 (94) is one that applies to us all: "If today you hear God's voice, harden not your hearts."

This possibility is especially strong if we approach the Scriptures only routinely. We let the words flow over us, "like water off a duck's back." We hear the Scriptures again and again but they make little impression on us. We are familiar with Jesus' words about forgiveness, for instance, yet we never allow them to address our particular conflicts. This attitude of resistance to any message that might convey a grace of conversion leads us to rationalize our unchristian behavior and effectively render God's word impotent.

It is the experience of many that *lectio divina* often leads to prayer later in the day. This will only happen if we allow the content of our sacred reading to linger on the outskirts of consciousness, ready to step inside when there is an opportunity. On the other hand, not remembering is often a means of protecting ourselves from the call to return to God. Prayer builds upon some antecedent willingness to reform our lives. To remain receptive to an invitation to unite ourselves with God in a moment of prayer is practically inseparable from allowing our daily conduct to be judged by God's word.[36] Refusal to be touched results in a certain hardness of heart that is the opposite of that quality of compunction that we discussed in the first chapter. Just as compunction helps us to be mindful of all that God has said and leads to prayer, so hardheartedness issues in forgetfulness and progressively isolates us from God, from amendment of life, and ultimately from our own truth.

Blindness. Sometimes we are sincerely ignorant of the reality of our own lives. We mean well, but our faculty of self-knowledge is disabled. For various reasons we unconsciously deny elements in our behavior that others readily perceive as inconsistent with our professed values. This fundamental lack of self-knowledge, often reinforced by a reluctance to entrust ourselves to the counsel of others, manifests itself in an inability to realize when the Scriptures are vitally applicable to our own situations. Instead, we tend to hear messages for other people. Having repressed the truth about our own lives, we then proceed to project onto others what we have denied in ourselves. Meanwhile, we remain safe and unsaved. This situation is addressed many times in the Prophets and the Gospels; it is not enough to hear the word, we have to implicate ourselves in the message. We do not take the content of *lectio divina* to heart because we do not know ourselves. Perhaps we are blind. Maybe it is the case that we are so filled with foreboding that we are merely afraid to open our eyes.

"Irrelevance." At times we so rigidly define our lives that we cease to be open to new perspectives. Anything that feeds into our current concerns is accepted as relevant; everything else is dismissed as of lesser importance. So many significant issues are put "on hold" because we do not feel it is necessary that we deal with them right away. As a result, we do not build the infrastructure on which "relevant" insights will depend. Perhaps we hear the word and understand it intellectually. Because we do not carry it around, bridges are not built between the text and daily life. Not everything is immediately relevant. Sometimes we have to juggle two apparently divergent themes in our minds until some sort of connectedness links them. Suddenly the next step becomes evident. It takes time and it demands of us the capacity to let God's word untidy our lives in the short term. If we can live with this divine chaos, it will eventually produce consistency and harmony not based on denial and repression, but coming from the courageous effort to eliminate whatever is incompatible with the following of Christ.

Defective memory of what we read is often more than harmless distraction or "forgetfulness." It can be an indication that the basic thrust of life is independent from our religious endeavors. We may try to be more than "Sunday Christians" but still have not accepted the consequences of submitting the totality of our lives to progressive evangelization. We hope to keep intact a small portion of heathen territory where our private authority is unquestioned. In this case we seem to have forgotten the pithy saying attributed to Saint John of the Cross: "A bird can be as securely restrained by a light cord as by a stout chain."

To live mindfully does not mean immediately becoming perfect. What is involved is an awareness of the truth of our being, shabby and fragmented as it is. Thus alerted, we can invest our limited energies, not in massive programs of self-improvement, but in trying to perceive where God's grace is leading us and then following that impulse. If each step we take is God's choice then it will be both possible and fruitful, though not necessarily in the manner we imagine. We may have to live for years in a state of dissatisfaction with ourselves, but this is the price we pay for coming to a substantial reliance on the action of God.

Our reading puts us into an initial contact with God's word and will. For this relationship to blossom we need to break down whatever barriers exist to keep God away from certain zones of our life. Like Mary, the mother of the Lord, we are invited to cherish the word and ponder it in our hearts (Luke 2:19). This is not merely a matter of dwelling on the hard truths that force us to avoid delusion. Mindfulness is also a matter of deliberately thinking about the positive components of faith and allowing ourselves to be influenced by them. The outcome of this is a life marked by hope and joy. As usual, Bernard of Clairvaux expresses this thought clearly:

> Therefore, my advice to you, friends, is to turn aside from troubled and anxious reflection on your own progress, and escape to the easier paths of remembering the good things God has done. In this way, instead of becoming upset by thinking about yourself, you will find relief by turning your attention to God ... Sorrow for sin is, indeed, a necessary thing, but it should not prevail all the time. On the contrary, it is necessary that happier recollections of God's generosity should counterbalance it, lest the heart should become hardened through too much sadness and so perish through despair.[37]

Remembering God's word is a comfort as well as a challenge. Inevitably it brings happiness because, in the last analysis, it is always good news. The lesson we learn from experience is that often the scriptural message needs to be held and ruminated so that its full sweetness can be savored. If we cut short our exercise of *lectio divina* and consider it finished when we close the book, then, almost certainly, we will receive from it less.

A final thought on the subject of mindfulness comes from John Cassian. Often when we become upset about something, our disturbance is caused by a lack of proportion in our assessment of issues. We attribute greater significance to some event or non-event and our resultant distress is worse than it has to be. Our reactions get out of control. We can gain some alleviation of this instinctive tendency to exaggerate our troubles by referring all situations to the fundamental principles of our faith. "All things work together to good for those who love God ... If God is with us, who can stand against us?" (Romans 8:28, 31). It is important that we do not allow peripheral issues to swamp our thoughts and lead us to desperation. God's love for us and the victory of Christ are realities worth recalling. This is the way Cassian speaks of this:

> Each hour and every moment we keep opening the ground of the heart with the plough of the gospel, that is, with the constant recalling of Christ's cross, and so we can eliminate the wounds inflicted by wild beasts and the bites of poisonous snakes.[38]

In other words, keeping the good news of Jesus Christ in mind helps us to avoid being overcome by the diminishment and pain from which no human life is exempt. Mindfulness of revelation is an active defense against disappointment and despair. And as such, it enhances our capacity to commit ourselves to what we believe in and to become tireless in doing good.

4

THE PRACTICE OF *LECTIO DIVINA*

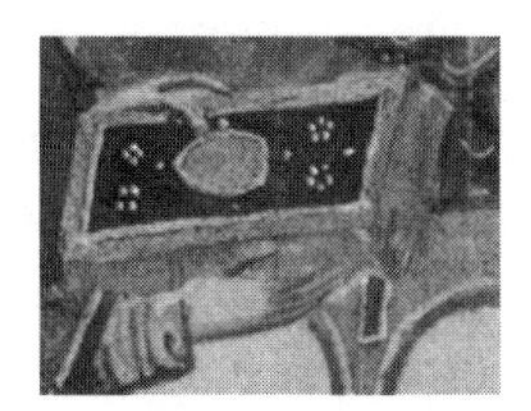

I have already written about the practice of sacred reading in my earlier book, *Toward God*. In this chapter I wish to enter into a little more detail and to say something about the specific difficulties we may encounter if we persevere in the practice for many years. Much of what was said at the beginning of this book about making time for *lectio divina*, paying attention during it, and remembering it afterward is relevant to practice. For the moment, however, I would like to leave general considerations aside and simply outline a typical scenario from which we might learn something.

It is probable that nobody will follow these suggestions absolutely. Nor is there any need to do so. This is a book for reflection, not a recipe book! Whatever I say has to be squared with a person's own experience and fitted into the possibilities that their life situation affords. It is important to have a balanced attitude about other people's practical suggestions. On the one hand, we need to be open to different possibilities, not only because our personal requirements change, but also because we have to accommodate ourselves to new circumstances as life unfolds. We have no guarantee that what worked well yesterday will continue to be useful tomorrow. On the other hand, it is good to be confident in our own experience and not to let our buoyancy be reduced by the weight of unfounded insecurities.

Translating theory into practice

Those who have persevered thus far with this book have probably begun to form some resolutions about upgrading their commitment to sacred reading. Like most resolutions these have only the faintest possibility of being remembered, much less implemented. The more comprehensive and expansive the resolution, the less likely it is that anything will come of it. From this perspective, it is probably better to begin with something simple.

On the basis of the principles enunciated in the first chapter, the best plan is to identify a brief daily slot that we could devote to sacred reading – with a backup, if necessary. The main thing is to be realistic. Lifelong exposure to God's word is more like a marathon than a sprint. It makes more sense to get something started in an imperfect state than to procrastinate forever. It is better for morale to spend five minutes once a day and stick with it, than to plan on a longer duration and fail to find time. Momentum will develop, and with the confidence that comes from success we can modify our tactics according to our experience.

If reading the Scriptures is a priority in our life then a regular slot in which we give ourselves gratuitously to *lectio* is imperative. A word of warning to those who deal professionally with the Bible. Don't attempt to double-up! If we are obliged to preach, teach, or study Scripture, it is important that this task-oriented reading does not displace a person-centered or call-oriented reading. And vice-versa. There will be inevitable overlaps, but the specific character of each exercise needs to be safeguarded. Slipping into study mode can be an insulation from challenges inherent in a text. Another temptation is to turn an incipient insight into a marketable commodity – a utilitarian attitude that may prevent me from staying longer with the text and plunging deeper. On the other hand, the requirements of objective interpretation do not allow me to intrude irrelevant personal agenda into an explanation or application intended for others. It may be the same Bible that we read in both instances, but there is a distinctive attitude that is appropriate to *lectio divina* that may elude us if we do not try consciously to cultivate it.

Many of the practical suggestions that are worth considering are means of highlighting the sacred character of *lectio*. Predictably, tactics that facilitate meditation often serve us well in building into our lives a regular segment of biblical reflection. I apologize if the following points seem obvious; it is my observation that it is often simple things that can make a change in the outcome of our efforts.

Ambience. If you do your *lectio divina* in areas associated with other activities, don't be surprised if you are assailed by distractions. Desk-workers will probably find that residual associations and memories associated with work will crowd in on our *lectio* when this is done at our desk. If we read in an armchair, we may begin to relax beyond what is helpful for serious attention. If we remember that we are subtly influenced by our environment, we may be motivated to experiment a little to discover a location that helps us remain alert and yet relatively free from opportunities of mind-wandering.[1]

The first requirement is a degree of privacy.[2] The Gospels tell us as much (Matthew 6:6). We are not on display, we want to avoid interruptions and have a little peace and quiet. Such a space is created by the convergence of three elements: a suitable location, a suitable time, and the cooperation of those with whom we live.

This means that some measure of planning and negotiation may be indicated. Going public in this way may be daunting to those who feel shy about their spiritual endeavors, but there are fringe benefits. Announcing our intentions to others can help us to be not only realistic in our planning but consistent in implementing what we decide.

The second requirement is illumination. Whereas meditation often works best in dimness, *lectio divina* obviously needs sufficient light to read the text comfortably. For some people a large-print Bible is a good idea.[3] Often some sort of bookstand can be helpful to get the page at the best angle and distance. Let each experiment to achieve the best results.

Some who spend a lot of time sitting find that to read standing is a pleasant change. As with meditation, those with more agile joints may find it useful to sit on the floor. This gives a different quality to the space around us. We can define an area temporarily by using a mat or cloth on the floor, or by adding a candle or some sacred symbol or icon. In this way we can create our own sacred site for the time of reading or meditation, and then return it to normal use when we are finished.

You may discover that the act of furnishing the place and occupying it focuses the mind and facilitates an interior sense of prayerfulness. The more quietly and consciously the preparations are made the easier the transition into a recollected state.

There are other ways of changing the environment. The use of fresh flowers, incense, or essential oils can add a pleasant fragrance to an otherwise ordinary place. I am in two minds about the value of using quiet background music. It can help to interpose a barrier between us and ambient cacophony, a sort of "white noise." I can see a role for music as a means of tranquillity and relaxation during a preparatory phase, but my opinion is that during the time of sacred reading itself, it is better to attempt to do it in silence. Especially for those more appreciative of music, it can be a distraction or a substitute for the task in hand. I say this diffidently; your own experience may lead you to another conclusion.

Ritual. Many people find that the repetition of customary actions is a great help in dropping off to sleep. As the time for bed approaches, the mind is put on autopilot and the degree of conscious involvement in activities is reduced. The same kind of process can often help us in our prayer-related activities. We begin to defer to another time the tasks that remain undone. This is the negative phase of moving into prayer or *lectio*: we place a temporary block on activities and concerns that belong to another part of the day. This is easier said than done, but it is not impossible. As this evacuation of thoughts proceeds we gradually turn our minds and hearts to the things of God.

In meditation and sacred reading it is useful to begin formally or with some measure of ritual. We may assume a particular posture to remind ourselves of what we are doing, or say some familiar prayer.

Inserting prayer. Sometimes prayer wells up naturally during our *lectio divina*; in such cases we do not need much external guidance. At other times our reading may seem dry; then we have to prime the pump. If no prayer rises spontaneously from the text, we have to make a positive effort to add prayer. If prayer is slow in coming, it makes sense for us to go out and meet it halfway.

At the beginning, we can introduce a prayerful element by consciously saying a prayer – especially one that asks God's assistance in the reading we are about to begin. We can do this spontaneously, or use a familiar formula, or perhaps make use of a liturgical prayer that attracts us.[4] Alternatively, we might like to begin with a psalm. We can take one of the sections of Psalm 119 (118); the whole psalm is a celebration of the gift of God's word, and saying part of it reflectively before we begin our reading helps instill in us that spirit of joyful reverence that makes us sensitive to its inner meaning.

During the reading too we should remember to pray. Let the text find an echo in our hearts so that we become part of the events that we read about. Sometimes the words of the text are directly applicable to our present situation and we can simply adopt them as a vehicle for our prayer. Thus, we may readily identify with the prayer of the publican (Luke 18:13) or the cry of the Canaanite woman (Matthew 15:22). Alternatively, what we read may arouse feelings, memories, and desires in us which express themselves naturally in other words or even in texts from different parts of the Bible. The discourse on the bread of life in the sixth chapter of John may cause us to pray "I do believe. Help my unbelief!" (Mark 9:24). Inevitably there will also be occasions when we turn the page unsuspecting and are suddenly overwhelmed by the intensity of the imagery. We discover aspects of our relationship with God that we scarcely knew existed. Passages like Isaiah 63–64, Jeremiah 20:7–18, or the Prayer of Azariah (Daniel 3:26–45 in Catholic Bibles) may be for us a powerful call to prayer and even the beginning of a renewal of fervor. In each case we have to allow the text to lead us, without fully understanding what our final destination will be. It is our willingness to let the Bible stimulate prayer in us that makes our reading a dynamic factor in our ongoing conversion. Without prayer, *lectio* is less *divina*; it becomes mere reading.

When our session of sacred reading draws to a close, we may wish to conclude with the Lord's Prayer, a short psalm of thanksgiving, or a prayer based on the passage we have just read. It is a simple means of effecting the transition from reading to life.

Active reading. If our normal reading has become no more than a rapid scanning of the page with a view to extracting its "essential" content, we will probably need to be re-educated if we are to improve our skills of sacred reading. *Lectio divina* is like reading poetry: we need to slow down, to savor what we read, and to allow the text to trigger memories and associations that reside below the threshold of awareness. We are so accustomed to reading quickly and "objectively" that we easily slip back into that habit, even when we are reading purely for "subjective" profit. This means that we may have to make a stand to protect the specific character of holy reading.

Being busy to establish good habits in *lectio divina* is an effective means of maintaining its distinctive character. One useful technique is to revert to the ancient practice of verbalizing as we read. This means that as we read a text we vocalize the words, saying them quietly to ourselves or even aloud. Doing this certainly slows us down. By adding sound to sight, reading aloud increases its power both to capture our attention and to evoke latent memories. It attunes us more fully to the poetic rhythms in which the Bible abounds. In the normal course of events it makes it easier to keep distracting thoughts at bay since it is almost impossible for the mind to drift towards alternative thoughts while we are actively vocalizing. It may seem an odd practice, but if you try it for yourself you may well become convinced of its utility.

Another ancient practice that is good both for attention and retention is to write out the texts that seem to speak more eloquently to us. This is not an acquisitive action, separable from the devout reading itself: a means of exploiting the text and carrying away elements that will be useful elsewhere. Writing out a text can be done in another way that makes it intrinsic to the reading and not an addition. The act of writing is itself a meditation – a way of assimilating what we read. We write carefully and reverently as a means of staying longer with the text and exploring its implications. As we do it, the word is imprinted more fully on our consciousness and there is a greater possibility that it will continue to exercise an influence over us in the future. We can write it on a small card to carry with us through the day or to leave in a place where we can see it. Alternatively, we may wish to compile a *florilegium* as the ancient monks did, writing a verse or two of our daily reading in a book, so that gradually we build up an anthology of texts that have spoken to us. Thus our reading can issue in a "*lectio* journal,"[5] that chronicles the history of our devotion to God's word. Two points we need to remember. Strictly speaking, we are referring to writing down passages of Scripture, without added comment or personal reflection. Such belong in another kind of journal. Secondly, the act of writing is as important as the end product. We should strive to write mindfully and with care. The practice should never become routine, but should always represent an act of homage and submission to a text that has begun to speak to us but which we would love to penetrate more.

Sacred reading is a way of spending time with God's revealed word: it involves reflection on the meaning of the text, application to our own situation and a willingness to be led into prayer. Sometimes it is helpful to institutionalize these elements to remind ourselves about the nature of the exercise we are engaged in. One way of doing this is to dialogue with the text as though it were a person, asking it questions and listening for responses within us. Many of the Fathers of the Church used this method on occasion as a means of teasing out the meaning of Scripture. If our mind is wandering, an exercise such as this can sometimes ease its restlessness. Such "discussion questions" are a little artificial and are not for use every time we read, but sometimes they can be helpful starters when nothing else seems to work.

Instead of questions we may prefer to spend some time writing a prayer based on the passage that we have just read. Having reflected on the text in the context of our life, we become aware of certain feelings and desires: these we address to God. We encapsulate the experience of a particular reading in a collect that we can use afterwards as a means of returning to that experience. As with the *lectio* journal, simplicity is the key. We will have little difficulty if we take the traditional model for a liturgical prayer, having three main elements:

[Address to God],
i Theme from the text (often refers to the past),
ii Petition drawn from the text (often refers to the present),
iii Development of the petition (often refers to the future),
[Conclusion].

Two examples may demonstrate this technique. If we had been reading of the events of the Exodus we might pray thus:

O God of all the living,
i When your people were hungry you fed them with manna.
ii Give us this day our daily bread
iii and may our trust in your providence never falter.
We ask this through Christ our Lord.

Alternatively, our reflection on Jesus' cleansing of the temple may lead us to formulate the following petition:

Lord Jesus Christ,
i You were consumed with zeal for the integrity of God's house.

ii Purify your Church from all that defiles and disfigures
iii and give us a clean heart so that we may see God.
For you are our Lord, forever and ever.

Apart from being a discipline that pushes us from reading to prayer, the writing of collects such as these also represents a shift from individual consciousness to a sense of solidarity. The word of God helps us not only to pray for our own needs, but to make intercession for all God's sons and daughters.

Avoiding drowsiness. If we are talking tactics then we need to say something about ways to avoid going to sleep during our reading. Because *lectio divina* takes place in a low-impact environment, it is easy to become drowsy, especially if we are tired or bored. There are a few commonsense precautions that we can take.

- Choose a time of the day in which we are less likely to be sleepy.
- Make sure that there is sufficient oxygen in the air to sustain wakefulness. Open a window; if you are using a portable heater, turn it off.
- Use a posture that is not too relaxed and encourages alertness.[6] A straight spine often helps.
- Don't stay too long. Prolonging reading beyond appropriate limits can be a cause of sleepiness.
- Recognize that we cannot do always what we can do sometimes; we have to be realistic in periods of diminished energy.
- Sometimes it helps to vary the content of our reading – for example to switch from one biblical book to another – so that a little variety acts as a break to the monotony.
- If none of these practical suggestions effects an improvement, it may be that our sleepiness is really passive resistance. Unconsciously we do not wish to attend to God's word. Perhaps we fear conversion! If such is the case we need to review our situation, and perhaps take counsel with someone whose wisdom we respect.

If sleepiness is occasional and clearly linked with special situations, it can be practically ignored. It happens to nearly everyone sometimes. If it occurs regularly then it is worth doing something about it. Time is too precious to waste in catnaps.

Corporate reading. It was the experience of the ancient monks that reading together was a good thing, whether this was a common reading or simply a matter of several reading privately in a common space. There is nothing to prevent husband and wife, family, group or community experimenting with different formats of reading together on either a temporary or permanent basis.

Such an exercise can accommodate different degrees of sharing, depending on the intimacy of those who take part. Maybe they simply inhabit a common space and time and read their own books. Perhaps they might begin or end with a general prayer. There may be an optional sharing of thoughts, feelings, and desires aroused in the reading. It is possible for there to be one book or many.

There is a value in corporate reading, but it is not absolute; it operates in function of the relationship existing among the participants. Where the practice of *lectio* seems endangered by a lack of support or stimulation, sometimes a corporate approach can provide an answer. Two or three gathered in the name of Christ are graced with his special presence. On the other hand, it is necessary that the participants come together freely. Any who feel pressured and constrained will probably derive little benefit from the exercise; the danger is that their outward conformity to expectations will generate an inner riot of imagination and feeling that will jeopardize any desirable outcome.

Whether these suggestions are of any help in individual cases, I would like to insist that all of us need to think about the practicalities of *lectio divina*. So often, a few basic precautions can make all the difference so that our good will and investment of time yield proportionate results. If our sacred reading serves as a channel of meeting with God, then it is far more likely that we will continue its practice. Conversely, reading that is perceived as not serving its purpose will be inevitably curtailed or abandoned.

When God seems silent

There have been many instances in history where persons have been spectacularly converted by the power of the scriptural word. You also, the reader, probably have some experience of how God gives light and strength through the medium of the sacred text. The impact of the Bible is especially powerful in the early days of discipleship, when we need to be alerted to a new way of living and gradually weaned from the gratifications of familiar heathen practice. In the low-impact landscape of our inner experience these moments are dramatic and so unpredictable as to appear divine. It is as though God seizes our attention through such minor cataclysms and begins to refashion our lives. We experience it as a spiritual rebirth or even as a new creation – thanks to the action of God's Spirit-filled word.

Significant as such moments are in our personal history of salvation, they are not normative for the whole of life.[7] Once our will is firmly attached to Gospel living a different dynamic is experienced. A different law is experienced in our members.[8] It is an example of what Aldous Huxley termed "induction" – the principle that "every positive begets its corresponding negative."[9] Any striving after a specific virtue issues in temptation against that virtue; every forward step is followed by an almost irresistible tendency to backslide. Practical decisions are based on calculated judgment, not on certainty; none is immune from doubts or regrets about hypothetical alternatives. An act of commitment does not change our reality. It is as though will and experience bound ahead of our total inner reality; as soon as we pause to take a breath we are overwhelmed by the negative inertia of our unevangelized zones. Instead of continuing our advance, we are forced to mount a rearguard action to secure our bases.

Almost by definition a honeymoon cannot last forever. The same is true of the practice of *lectio divina,* as it is in prayer and in every other human endeavor. Initial enthusiasm gives way to a more seasoned equanimity, where the emphasis is on growing in faith and fidelity. As progress is made, we come to our reading of sacred Scripture less for gratification than out of a conviction that it is a good thing to live according to the Gospel. This "obedience of faith," as Saint Paul terms it (Romans 1:5, 16:26), is a very mature and long-lasting spiritual attitude. It indicates that we have assented to our being created anew in the likeness of Jesus Christ. This is what we believe. At the level of feeling we may experience more the preliminary work of deconstruction. There is no cheap grace, nor can any inner rottenness be hidden from the eye of our all-caring surgeon. We cannot measure the effectiveness of a spiritual discipline by the comfort it brings – only by its results, and these are in the future.

It is no bad sign when we lose the superabundance of pleasure we once had in *lectio divina*. It is a habitual indication that we have passed beyond the beginnings. At this stage we have two species of demons to contend with. First we have to struggle to maintain our openness to God's word and to remain faithful to regular exposure to it. Secondly, and this may come as a surprise, we have to contend with our own inner outrage as our deep resistances to revelation become disinhibited. Often we are astonished and confused because we never expected a pious practice to lead to the experience of such strong contrary inclinations. Yet God's word and Spirit lead us ineluctably to the truth, and part of that truth is that there is much within us that is resistant to God's love. Only when we become conscious of this do we truly seek God, and thereby open ourselves to the healing balm of divine mercy.

So, easy accessibility to God's word gives way to a "famine of the word" (Amos 8:11–12). Not the daily alternation that marks all our activities but a chronic sense that we are drifting away from God and no longer able to hear the divine voice. False solutions present themselves readily. We are tempted to abandon our regular practice of sacred reading and let our intensity of spiritual life wind down. Alternatively, we may attempt to blast through the wall by will power and endurance; this way we eventually exhaust ourselves and the effect is equally uncreative. What is called for is a stolid perseverance while we are gradually changed, accepting that nothing is wrong with the reading itself. We have simply entered a new phase, and time is needed before we feel comfortable in it.

It is as though God is speaking to us in a new language. We need to sit quietly for a time and let the words flow over us. Soon some sense will begin to emerge from the confusion and new light will illumine the landscape of our hearts. We are being re-educated and our spirits are slowly being attuned to the subtle harmonies of God. What we experienced as the breakdown of all we had hitherto acquired in sacred reading is now perceived as a transition. The transcendent mystery constantly calls us to go beyond our comfortable limits, to let our hearts be expanded so that they may more fully accommodate God.

It is hard to find words that are sufficiently anti-dramatic to describe this change. However I describe it, such a transition appears as a high-powered experience. Your own experience in this regard is probably less spectacular. It combines elements of distraction, disappointment, discouragement. You notice a tendency to cut corners and invest less in sacred reading; boredom and irritation surface during it and a restlessness that wants us to be somewhere else. We forget to read and we forget what we read. Prayer becomes perfunctory and God seems absent. In this situation it is not surprising that we either fall back to former ways or become the prey of new demons striking out from our unconscious.

The eighteenth-century hymnographer William Cowper addresses this situation in the hymn, "O for a closer walk with God":

> Where is the blessedness I knew
> when first I saw the Lord?
> Where is the soul-refreshing view
> of Jesus and his word?[10]

Cowper is speaking here of a common experience. For this reason, it is important to ask ourselves *why* God seems silent. Without a diagnosis of our condition, no remedy or response is likely to help. It has long been recognized that there are different causes of such a sense of tedium; if we know what factors are operative in our own case we will have a better chance of doing something to improve the situation. Here I give some general indications.

Ill health. Illness often upsets the equilibrium of the whole organism; even a mild bout of flu can render our normal spiritual exercises impracticable. More serious and prolonged ailments also undermine our efforts, especially if they are undiagnosed or their effects not understood.

In such cases we have to learn to live within our limits and not uselessly to strive against them. We should always consider the possibility that our difficulties in *lectio divina* are not the results of deficient will power but of some physical disability. Here we have to learn to accept reality graciously. If our attention span is very short or we find it very difficult to concentrate, then we need to experiment with brief – and perhaps more frequent – blocks of time. If our sight is impaired we will need to get new spectacles, find a large-print

Bible, try listening to tapes, or have someone read to us. Some radical simplification of the content of our reading may be indicated: it might be better, for example, to stay with the Gospels. God's word is conducive to our well-being and should never be permitted to lapse fully, even though some ingenuity may be needed to devise ways of availing ourselves of it when our faculties are impaired. It is not my competence to be able to make recommendations for those who suffer from some degree of dyslexia. I merely record the existence of such a condition and express the hope that professionals involved in the area can suggest appropriate remedies.

Lack of training. Because most of us live in a literate society, it is easy to assume that to get persons started on *lectio divina* it is sufficient to give them a Bible and tell them to begin reading. We may have suggestions on *what* to read, but we often do not think it necessary to tell them *how* to read or to inform them of the ways sacred reading differs from the common perusal of a book or magazine.[11] To some extent this book is intended to meet this need. This is what has been learned in centuries of monastic experience; try some of it and you may find it helpful! Creating a prayerful space that accords with our personal rhythm of life does not come naturally. We need instruction and reflection to find something that suits and, even then, nurturing and monitoring is necessary to ensure that our activity does not become an end in itself. What we do should not be the primary focus of our energies; our spiritual exercises should progressively become so transparent that God shines through them.

Social disharmony. God's word is unitary; it cannot be simultaneously welcomed and rejected. It is useless to embrace Christ in prayer or *lectio* and then to spurn him in our brothers and sisters. The message of Matthew 25 holds good not only for the final judgment; it also applies to our experience in sacred reading. Any failure to seek Christ, any reluctance to receive him, will be reflected in our experience of *lectio divina*. We who pray "forgive us as we forgive" cannot afford to live in a state of conflict with others. To the extent that our will is not active in seeking resolution and reconciliation, the fundamental attitude required for sacred reading is defective and its fruits will be proportionately meager.

Pedagogical withdrawal. Our sacred reading, like our prayer, often reflects what occurs at the level of behavior. Sometimes the reason *lectio divina* seems to be going nowhere is to be sought in specific choices made by us that constitute a step away from God. An overt act of injustice or unchastity, the breaking of a commitment, the refusal of obedience, or calculated nastiness to a neighbor can bring to nothing years of apparent progress. God withdraws from us and allows us to experience the extent of our own unlovableness. It is as though God suspends the relationship to demonstrate an unwillingness to become an accomplice in our crime. Deliberate un-Christlike behavior is necessarily a turning away from God; without repentance we cannot continue as before.

Yet too often, instead of being sorry for what we have done, we resort to rationalization. We sincerely believe and frequently affirm that we have done nothing wrong.[12] To lead us to repentance, God has first to break through the husk of falsehood and complacency. Since we are unwilling to learn, God withdraws and leaves us to our fate.

Such an abandonment is pedagogical and not vindictive. As Saint John Chrysostom remarks in the context of the Prodigal Son, "When words would not convince us, God often leaves us to learn from the things that happen to us."[13] The silence of God in this case is an eloquent condemnation of an unholy act of will on our part. The change in our experience is meant to help us recognize the truth of what we have done and to take imaginative steps to repair the damage. When, like the Prodigal Son, we "return to ourselves" and begin to retrace our tracks, then God's silence is replaced by words of peace and acceptance, and a great celebration ensues. We are not rejected by God – only our ugly actions; when we separate from them, the covenant of friendship is resumed.

Seasonal variations. All human reality passes through different seasons. In God's dealings with us there is a time for both speech and silence (Ecclesiastes 3:7). Sometimes God's silence is an indication that we are not in a position to listen. Like the ancient Israelites, we are overcome with dread at the prospect and cry out, "Let not God speak to us, lest we die" (Exodus 20:19). We need time to accustom ourselves to the new demands that God's call imposes on us. We have to work through our instinctive resistance until we reach the point at which we can say in all honesty, "Speak, Lord; your servant is listening" (1 Samuel 3:9). God does not speak before we are ready; meanwhile, we are left to ourselves to ponder in silence.

As we advance in familiarity with God's word, the progression is interrupted once or twice by major qualitative changes, often linked with the "obscure nights" that Saint John of the Cross chronicled. The secure synthesis that we had elaborated is subject to deconstruction. Our system fails. Fragmentation sets in, and we are left with a sense of having achieved nothing. In this confused state we learn again the lesson of dependence on God, and so we begin once more. In these transitions God's silence is more profound and we are left longer in it. More radical, too, are the changes in perspective to which we must submit, if we are to hear again the subtle melodies of the Spirit.

Divine transcendence. All these elements represent different manifestations of two complementary truths: on the one hand, the mystery of God, on the other, the radical incapacity of human beings. The Bible is more than a book; it is the revelation of ultimate reality. No matter how feeble the human language of the Bible, it is our faith that it mediates the self-disclosure of God. When we approach the sacred Scriptures we are not merely reading or studying one book among many. We are being confronted with the mystery that transcends all intellect and surpasses our skills. We can never master the Bible, in the sense of conquering it. The most we can do is to submit to it. "Receive with meekness the word that has been sown, for it has power to save your souls" (James 1:21). Without humility we cannot penetrate God's word. "God resists the proud and gives grace to the humble" (James 4:6; 1 Peter 5:5; see Proverbs 3:34). When, like Job, we recognize the futility of human contestation with God, we can begin to "repent in dust and ashes" (Job 42:6). It is at this point that we are probably most open to receive from God the full weight of revelation.

These are the main reasons why God can seem silent when we attempt to read the Scriptures. Some of these situations admit of simple solutions, others demand some effort from us either to do or to endure. The point is to know that silences will ensue in our reading and to have some capacity to gauge their causes.

One source of our inability to extract a message from our reading remains to be mentioned. It is so important that it deserves a section to itself. We fail to hear God because there is too much noise within.

Inner noise

Some of what we will say on this matter will overlap with what was said in the previous section or elsewhere in this book. For the sake of clarity, however, a little repetition may be tolerable. As elsewhere, I am attempting to describe the common experience of serious readers of the Scriptures; some elements will be more relevant than others to particular present situations.

The largest obstacle that prevents our hearing the word of God is the volume of interior noise that interferes with our perception. Even when we slow down and cease from other activities, we do not easily enter into a state of expectant listening. Often the reverse is true. It is only when we quiet down exteriorly and disengage from engrossing occupations that we realize what a wild riot of potential disturbances exists within. I will try to describe some of the principal sources of this cacophony.

Residual echoes. Most of us have come to accept that it is normal to live in a noisy environment and have little appreciation for the value of physical silence. Radio, television, and tapes, are the usual accompaniment of life. By our choice of them we create a cocoon of personal space that we find comforting. Our sounds are music; the sounds of others are noise. If the sounds around us are not of our own making, we blot them out by adding more or increasing the volume of our own. Aural stimulation is such a necessary part of modern life that many cannot handle silence. There are some who fear silence, as children fear the dark. Once their thoughts are no longer prompted externally, deeper thoughts may surface and they are afraid of the result of that unaccustomed process. So they attempt to frighten away the ghosts with noise: clatter, conversation, and the cheerful inanities of media entertainment.

Continual ambient noise tends to leave a residue within us – an after-image, as it were. If we have been working with noisy equipment, our whole organism continues to vibrate long after work ceases. Generally, whenever we attempt to be quiet, the echoes of half-heard sounds make their presence felt: jingles and snatches of music dance at the edge of consciousness, we find ourselves urgently trying to remember a word of no consequence, conversations and conflicts are relived.[14] There are two possible messages to draw from this experience.

The first is that we need to consider the possibility of making our normal environment less abrasive. Learning to live quietly is a means to a richer life. It helps us both to concentrate on what we are doing and remain open to inspiration. Working noisily, on the other hand, is often an expression of passive aggression or rebellion, and constantly half-listening to the radio can indicate boredom and distaste for what we are doing. Hyperstimulation can only be remedied by reducing the volume. It is worth trying. There is a lot of healing to be found in silence – at least for those who are mature and well-adjusted.

The second message is this. To the extent that we are unwilling or unable to modify our environment, it may be necessary to think in terms of giving ourselves time to detoxify before attempting meditation or reading. To move towards a state of inner composure it is often better to create a space in which our aural phantasms surface naturally and disappear, rather than to dissipate our energies trying to shoo them away while we read. Perhaps we need to redefine for ourselves the meaning of relaxation so that noise is not part of it.

If noise is a significant element in our lives, then probably some of it will be internalized. In that case we will experience the after-effects of a noisy environment whenever we open ourselves to sacred reading. To close off that potential avenue of disruption, some common-sense, practical measures may well need to be embraced.

Acedia. Acedia is a state in which we find it impossible to commit ourselves to any serious and sustained activity. We have discussed it briefly in the first chapter of this book (p. 19). There is something inside us that makes us jumpy and restless and unable to pay attention to anything for long. The causes of this condition are manifold and in serious cases need professional attention. One who is unable to settle down to reading cannot be receptive of God's word. Such people will be driven by their instability of mind to act out whatever comes into their thoughts from sources deep within their personality. So great will be the interference that not even the semblance of sacred reading seems possible. Saint Aelred of Rievaulx draws this picture of an acediac monk:

> You know, brothers, that silence is a burden for many. Quiet weighs them down. As a result, everything becomes a burden when they have to stop speaking and be quiet: their head aches, their

> stomach rumbles, they cannot see, their kidneys weaken ... You may see a monk sitting in the cloister, looking this way and that, yawning frequently, stretching his arms and legs. Now he puts the book down. Now he takes it up again. Finally, as if stung by a goad, he gets up and wanders from place to place, and from one parlor to another.[15]

Once we have identified such restlessness within ourselves, we can ask ourselves whether we want to be dominated by it. The classical remedy for acedia was to remain steadfastly in one's cell. Even if we cannot diagnose the cause of acedia or prescribe a remedy, we still have the power to stay where we are and to persevere in our efforts. Such resolution often does the trick.

Overconcern with external projects. Saint Luke draws a very clear picture of the potential conflict between fussy concern with things-to-be-done and quiet listening to the Lord (Luke 10:38–42). We are aware from our own experience that there is a sort of concern that produces fragmentation. We all know people who are easily flustered. A loss of perspective sets in and the ultimate goal of existence gradually fades from awareness.

The New Testament repeatedly rejects this narrowing species of care as an equivalent to a failure of trust. There is a niggling sense of insecurity that keeps telling us that we should be doing more. We will soon find that we have less opportunity for reading and meditation if we allow the practical agenda to dominate our lives. At some point we have to make a stand. If time and energy are constantly extroverted we become strangers in our own inner world. We do not feel at home in stillness and receptivity. As a result, our quiet times are progressively eroded both qualitatively and quantitatively in favor of activity.

It is amazing how productive our imaginations can be as soon as we try to pray or read. Urgent things that need to be done yesterday clamor for our attention. Mostly we need to ignore them. Did I turn on the washing machine? Instead of running to check, ask yourself what is happening here. Don't be forced into immediately abandoning your reading, but think it over for a moment and make an adult choice. If we do not agree indiscriminately to such intrusions, they will happen less frequently. A small notebook can be useful to write down any bright ideas that seem likely to continue; we mark them down for future action and dismiss them as inappropriate for this time.

It is easy for the brief span in which we give ourselves to *lectio* to be hijacked by other concerns. To some extent this will be inevitable if we live an unprocessed life. All we can do during the time of reading is to refuse to be lightly budged from our serious occupation. There are still plenty of hours in the day to do what has to be done.

Divided heart. If singleness of heart is a factor in arriving at a spiritual understanding of the Scriptures, it must be clear that those with a "double soul" (James 1:8; 4:8) will often experience the revealed word as impenetrable. It is the undivided heart that finds God in the Bible. To the extent that vast areas of our life are inconsistent with the faith we profess, an inner battle rages that blocks out the still, small voice of God. There may be nothing wrong with the text that we scan or our intellectual formation, but the Bible will remain remote from us when we try to serve two masters. The Scriptures are meant for disciples. The more we have the attitude of disciples the more we will learn.

On the other hand, a benefit that comes with the regular reading of the Bible is that we are brought face to face with the superficiality of our existing commitment. It is easy to believe that our lives are inspired by the Gospels if we keep the Gospels at a distance. Only closer scrutiny of the text challenges this complacency and reveals much in us that is unevangelized. This information is the first step in addressing the interior division that is blocking our understanding. In this way, the difficulty, correctly diagnosed, already points the way to its own resolution. The word of God brings us to the point of a more comprehensive decision that, in turn, clears the way to a deeper understanding. And not only that. Subpersonal forces disable the powers of perception by creating zones of disharmony within us. When we recognize this stratagem and strive to neutralize it with God's help, three things follow: our house is at peace, our vision is unclouded, and our ears begin to hear God speak in the Scriptures. At this point we come to appreciate that "disciple" and "discipline" are related concepts. We cannot be true followers of Christ without a rule of life that leads the primal chaos within us toward obedience to God's creative word.

Alienation from the Church. In the previous part of this chapter we listed "social disharmony" among the causes of God's apparent silence. Here I would like to speak about a specific form of this that often makes itself felt during sacred reading.

There are those who seek from the Church a perfection that they would never demand of individuals. Bitterness sets in when their dream is unrealized; they centrifuge and become more and more marginal. Any attempt at meditation or reading often leads to a rehearsal of their private log of grievances. The Scriptures speak to them only of the inadequacies of others, reinforcing their sense of victimhood and inspiring in them an eloquence to denounce that does not come from God.

That this is not sacred reading is apparent from its fruits. Patience and tolerance are needed if we are to survive within the Church. When these are lacking the great benefits of word, sacrament, and communion that are the essential dynamism of ecclesial life are forgotten. Politics and personal pique rule instead. Sacred reading cannot thrive in such a climate.

Unconscious factors. Many of these inner sources of static are unconscious. We do not want them to exist, we may not even be aware that they are operative. There is a resistance to God in all of us. Even though we believe that we are Christians and want to be, most of us have not yet radically submitted our will to God. Without an antecedent willingness to be instructed and to change, our reading of the Scriptures becomes selective. Faith is an obedience; we will not hear if we are unwilling to obey. Because we are good people who could not countenance rebellion against God, our zest for autonomy is driven underground. It is still active, but we are serenely unaware that anything is wrong. It is like a virus in its incubation period; for the moment it is invisible, its effects barely noticeable except for a lower level of vitality. But there is always the possibility that one day there will be a spectacular eruption.

In this book I have tried to present *lectio divina* as a source of life and renewal. As such we may experience a distaste for this source of grace. It sometimes happens that we go through a phase of self-hatred and even self-destructiveness. Even if we are not brought to the point of doing violence to ourselves, this proclivity can nevertheless make us reluctant to avail ourselves of what would bring life. For no apparent reason we develop an aversion to what is healthy and healing, such as exercise, good diet, or new activities. We buttress this unconscious decision with the opinions of all sorts of experts and with facile rationalization. The truth, however, is that something inside us does not want to be helped along the way.

The same dynamism is apparent in the spiritual life. We back off from what would support our Christian commitment and subtly encourage those forces that undermine it. This can continue unsuspected for years. When the time for external decision arrives, the outcome is already fixed. We can do no other. Once the point of no return is passed, no blame can be laid. We have responded to the data; we have made the "right" decision. Perhaps. The real drama probably took place long before "the decision." Once we allow ourselves to drift, then the only possibility is that we drift downstream – even though bad faith and passivity sometimes obscure the radical nature of that choice. In this context many people wander away from the integral practice of sacred reading long before a crisis is evident. When the climax comes they find that they have drifted too far for *lectio divina* to be of any benefit. They have long since cut themselves off from what might have been of great assistance in difficult times. Yet they are substantially unaware of what has happened.

This is not the place to discuss the various psychological disorders that operate in such situations, nor have I the competence. Such unconscious factors operate to some extent in all of us and inhibit our sensitivity to spiritual reality by superimposing on everything our own hidden agenda. This is why most religious traditions value the practice of taking counsel: to verify the authenticity of our impulses, to seek to uncover our native blind spots, and to profit from the presence of the Holy Spirit in the heart of a fellow-believer. Inevitably, some cases, although they present religious symptoms, are more appropriately dealt with by a psychologist.

A chapter like this that deals with practical matters has to include a certain amount of trouble-shooting. When things are going well, who needs guidance? I am not suggesting that all these potential problems are universal or that a desire to live in fidelity to the Scriptures will necessarily founder on one of them. I think that if we are going to remain faithful to *lectio divina* throughout life, it is good for us to know the pitfalls so that we can avoid them. As with everything else I say, I expect you, the reader, to be discriminating. Take what is helpful for you at the moment, and let the rest flow over you.

Our *lectio divina* should not be so holy that we fear to view our practice with common sense and a critical eye. If it is not going well let us not be afraid to experiment. There may be nothing wrong. It may simply be that our circumstances have changed. It may also be that we have matured in our practice of sacred reading and are being called to a more challenging level of discipleship. Where there is life, there is growth. And with growth, change is inevitable.

5

READING TRADITIONAL AND PATRISTIC TEXTS

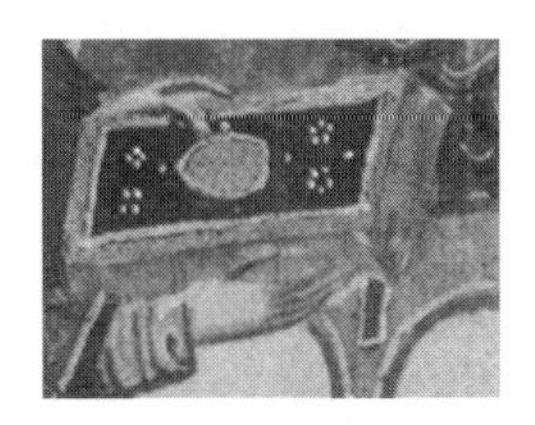

Up to this point I have been talking about the manner in which *lectio divina* has been done according to the Western tradition. It is now time to talk about its subject matter. For reasons of clarity I have, until now, concentrated on reading the Bible, which is sacred reading *par excellence*. But I would not like to leave the impression that only the Bible is appropriate for this exercise. The benedictine tradition is broad and not doctrinaire. Monastic experience throughout the centuries points to another channel of scriptural meditation: the living Bible that is the ongoing life of the Church.

Here we must remind ourselves of the essential nature of *lectio divina*. It is reading done under the aegis of the "obedience of faith." The purpose of *lectio* is to bring us to the point where we freely give the assent of faith in a manner that is progressively more profound and in continuity with the experience of everyday life. The matter of sacred reading must be such that it can sustain in us a sense of reverence and submission. It must be such that we can safely suspend our critical faculties and freely lay bare our soul to be moved.

Without denying to God the possibility that other channels of speech may be used, normally what we read for *lectio* should express the perennial faith of the Church and not the transient opinions of an individual. This present book, for instance, aims to present the monastic experience of sacred reading for your instruction and profit. It is not, however, a pure distillation of the tradition; in it are mixed also the opinions, prejudices, and experiences of its author. These may or may not be interesting, but they are certainly not normative for all. This means that I expect people to read with discernment, constantly verifying what I say against their own knowledge and experience and finally arriving at their own conclusions. So I offer this book for their critical attention. I rely on it. I would write very little if I thought readers were going to regard it as "gospel truth." By the time I filtered out my personal idiosyncrasies, I am sure there would be almost nothing left.

There is scope for reading that is not *lectio*. Those of us who are professionally mixed up with religion are obliged to keep somewhat abreast of current developments in several associated fields. It is good for all believers to know some theology and to understand a little about spirituality. Many people find themselves drawn to more evangelical behavior by coming into contact with the life of someone holy. Good religious biography is a source of much encouragement and teaching. For many of us without the opportunity of personal instruction by a spiritual guide, reading books is the only way we can get the information we need for continuing growth. Yes, there is scope for "spiritual reading," but it is not, strictly speaking, *lectio divina* – even though sometimes it comes close.

Appropriate matter of sacred reading is what expresses the perennial faith of the Church. In my understanding this would include liturgical texts, select writings of the Fathers (and Mothers) of the Church, the eminent teachers (or "Doctors") of the past (such as Teresa and John of the Cross) and some of the mystics (Julian of Norwich, the author of *The Cloud of Unknowing*, Meister Eckhart). For Roman Catholics there are many official documents of the *magisterium* that are fine for meditation and prayer: Council texts (especially Vatican II), some papal encyclicals and so forth. Some sections of the new *Catechism of the Catholic Church* are suitable for *lectio divina*. These are the less controversial sections that aim at helping readers make their faith more explicit and become aware of a more insistent call to holiness and union with God. The long section on prayer, although the style is elliptic, contains much that is enlightening and inspiring and could be read profitably by almost anyone.

Texts of tradition do not replace Scripture. They offer a profitable complement to the Bible, helping us to understand and apply its teaching. The Holy Spirit did not cease being active in the Church with the writing of the last page of the New Testament. Throughout the centuries the Spirit and the word have so infused the lives of countless men and women that they themselves became living gospels; the wisdom God gave them made apparent what was latent in the Scriptures. Such insights were not automatically guaranteed. It was only when generations of believers found in them accurate reflections of their own spiritual experience that these secondary texts began to have some measure of *auctoritas* – a word usually translated as "authority" but probably better rendered "prestige." Just as a good preacher can make the inspired word come alive for those who hear, so reading these classical Christian treatises can help translate the Bible from the past of history to the present of our own lives.

Patristic *lectio*

Among the thousands of authors that collectively constitute Christian tradition, those who are called "the Fathers of the Church" occupy a position of special importance.[1] There are several reasons for this.

First, the earliest Fathers, in particular, are considered to be witnesses of a very primitive species of Christianity. Second-century authors, for example, often provide insight into the custom and usage reflected in the New Testament. In general, the earlier authors are valued because they are more proximate beneficiaries of the apostolic tradition.

Taken collectively, the Fathers of the Church also help us to understand our own roots: where many beliefs and practices current in the later Church have their source and how they developed. The fact that they are far from unanimous on many issues is a comforting example of theological pluralism.[2] In this they are a precious aid in assessing the legitimacy of our own particular theological stance.

Another reason for their importance is that nearly all the Church Fathers had pastoral responsibilities. They wrote to help people come to grips with the teaching of Christ. As far as I know, theology was not seen as a profession or occupation in the first millennium. It was considered more as a concomitant of pastoral care, an essential component of the office of the bishop and his helpers. Saint Benedict, likewise, demanded that abbots and other officials be chosen not only for their exemplary lives, but for their ability to communicate to others the values by which they lived. Texts written from such a perspective tend to be existential, experiential, and practical. Theory is not allowed to run loose. So much heresy was simply a matter of one aspect of the truth taken to extremes, whereas pastoral concern restrains theory within the bounds of moderation.

Finally, in general, holiness of life and orthodoxy of doctrine were prerequisites to inclusion among the Church's venerated teachers. Without any official intervention like canonization, the process of acceptance was more informal. Only those were considered suitable who did not deviate from the faith of the Church, who practiced what they preached, and who were found acceptable as teachers by subsequent generations of the faithful.

The Church Fathers do more than explain the Bible. They offer us the fruits of their own spiritual experience. We who live at the end of two millennia of Christian faith can profit from what our forebears have learned. We do not have to keep beginning at ground level. This is especially true when it comes to teaching for the spiritually mature. The ancient Church recognized the distinction between *catechesis* and *mystagogia*. The former was for beginners, the later for those struggling with the different difficulties that follow some progress. There are many subjects treated only generally in the New Testament that are later developed more fully.

Translating the Gospels into a practicable rule of life. The monastic rules do this for monks; for layfolk, some adaptation is necessary. In addition there are letters of direction and sermons that offer valuable guidelines, although addressed to various particular circumstances.

Understanding the dynamics of virtue and vice. Most of us want to be good but often get tripped up because we do not understand how temptation creeps up on us. In this the teaching of Evagrius of Pontus, John Cassian, and Gregory the Great offer us a "spiritual psychology" that enables us to respond more fully and freely to the call of the Gospel. One of the things that will surprise us about the Fathers of the Church is the amount of attention they pay to the recipient of grace, that is, to the human factors that operate in the work of salvation.

Discernment. Many good people go astray because their zeal is without understanding (see Romans 10:2). Enthusiasm has a tendency to get carried away and so we are in need of moderating influences. One of the most important contributions of Christian tradition is to give guidance in spiritual discernment on the basis of sound experience.

Development. Christian discipleship is not static. As the Gospel parables of growth indicate, our following of Christ goes through different stages in the course of a lifetime. An understanding of the practical dynamics of spiritual progress helps us to respond more fully to the changing demands that God's call makes on us. Here "the science of the saints" can facilitate matters. When Saint John of the Cross describes and explains the "obscure nights" that mark important transitions in our lives, he is transmitting to us a wisdom generated over centuries that is contained in germ in the Bible but is neither explicit nor detailed.

Mystical union. The Gospel of John has much to say about "remaining" in God, and Saint Paul often refers to our being "in Christ." The experiential aspects of such realities are not, however, developed in the New Testament. Those whom grace leads to contemplative union will find encouragement and instruction in the writings of many who have walked the same way. In this matter, too, the writings of the Church Fathers and Mothers will help us both to be faithful to the grace given us and to penetrate the realities that Scripture refers to only in veiled and subtle terms.

Writings that are cherished by the Church offer us the means of gleaning some wisdom from those whom the providence of God has sent as teachers. But there is more. Because books were rare before printing, only manuscripts of value were copied. This meant that a process of filtration was going on that strained out authors or works considered of less value. In the history of selection, those texts became most known and loved that had the greatest capacity to foster genuine gospel living. The proportion of nonsense was considerably less than might be found in publishers' lists today.

Even so, we have to be selective in what we choose for sacred reading. Not everything preserved will serve us for prayerful reflection. To be suitable for *lectio divina* a book needs more than a guarantee of truth. I cannot here attempt to formulate universal principles. All I can do is to make explicit some of the elements involved in my personal practice. Before I attempt to find *lectio* in the writings of the Church Fathers, for instance, I would instinctively look for some of the following qualities.

A certain affinity with the author. For some reason I am attracted by certain figures of antiquity but not all. Though I am open to make the acquaintance of new authors, I enjoy most and profit from those whom I tend to regard as old friends. Bernard of Clairvaux,

Augustine of Hippo, and Julian of Norwich are among those whom I greatly cherish. Other favorites are listed at the end of this chapter. Different people will, inevitably, have a different list.

A work of experience. Mostly I seek books that speak about the experiential aspects of Christian life. Not pure exposition of the biblical text nor technical theology, but writing that stems from commitment and experience. So often those whose works are preserved were spiritual giants. When they write from experience there is a potency that far surpasses our own limits. We are surprised by what they see and we have missed. In a very true sense, they "open the Scriptures" to us, leading us to a level of understanding that we would never have attained unaided. Inevitably, there is a certain passion about such works that nudges them towards the poetic. I must admit that I have a predilection for literary quality. Being lucky enough to have acquired a facility in some of the relevant languages, I try to read these texts in the original. I feel that this also brings me closer to the author and to the experience that is the source of the text. The sense of reality that accompanies such contact makes a much stronger impact than mere abstract theory.

Appropriate subject matter. In reading the Fathers I have the liberty to choose from a vast range of topics whatever suits my current spiritual needs. I can read Cyprian on patience, Augustine's letter to Proba on prayer, or select a commentary on John by Origen or Chrysostom. In this way I can seek enlightenment in an area which is relevant to my life at present, or, as an alternative, choose to read something distinct from usual concerns as a means of keeping in touch with broader reality.

Appropriate genre. Not everything that even favorite authors write is suitable for sacred reading. Even the most pyrotechnic of the ancient masters occasionally produced a few duds. Polemic treatises I always eschew; no matter how true the positions espoused, the content is not expressed in a style that is conducive to prayerful reflection. I must admit that dense theology is a bit too much for me. It may be truthfully said at my funeral, "Imagine, he lived all those years and never read all of Augustine's *De Trinitate*!" The kind of writing that most often suits me is the sermon – mainly because sermons are usually based on particular texts of the Bible, proceed by relating these texts to others, and then draw lessons relevant to everyday behavior. Many who find themselves quickly bogged down in *The City of God* will be entranced and enthused by the directness of many of Augustine's sermons to the people.

Author and subject matter are important, but the purpose of writing also has a bearing on a particular text's palatability. The choice of genre, as we know, usually dictates the style and language of the work, and gives it a specific "feel." Before investing time in a particular book, it makes sense to determine first whether its genre is suitable for the purposes of *lectio divina*. If a work is too argumentative or abstruse, if its contents are too much linked to particular circumstances, we may well find that it becomes hard for us to enter into the spirit of the discussion or derive much profit from it, especially at the beginning of our acquaintance.

Culture shock. One of the factors that I appreciate in reading ancient authors is that they come from a distant culture. This means they build on a distinctive infrastructure of beliefs and values. When they comment on a text or discourse on a value, they approach things from a different angle and so often have something original to say. This is not to assert that their cultural values were necessarily better than ours. It simply means that they were more aware of some aspects of truth than we are – just as we know more than them in some matters. When we have recourse to writers of antiquity, we have the opportunity to compensate for the blind spots inherent in our particular culture. They help us move toward a more integral wisdom by challenging many of our presuppositions. Because they are unaffected by our particular cultural bias, they can help liberate us from the invisible ideology inherent in our uncritical assumptions about the nature of reality.

I insist that these are my personal criteria. I do not know how valid they might be for other people. Experience helps a lot in finding suitable works that can be absorbed with a similar openness and docility that we bring to our reading of the Bible.

Reading the Fathers is not always easy. Nor is it to be recommended indiscriminately to everyone. At the same time, there are many people who have spent years in faithful *lectio divina* on the Bible who may feel the need for "something different." These I would encourage to try using the skills they have developed in reading the Bible in approaching suitable texts from tradition. There are two requirements that we will quickly discover for ourselves: patience and instruction.

Patience is necessary because there is much about the Church Fathers that is foreign to us and, at the beginning, we do not have the same level of familiarity with them that we have attained with the Bible. If we belong to those for whom immediate gratification is a priority, then much patristic writing will be frustrating for us. Even Saint Benedict recognized this. At the end of his Rule for monasteries he offers a reading list. Of the Scriptures he says, "What page or word of divine authorship in the Old and New Testaments is not a most straight guide for human life?" Every word of the Bible can help us live well. Of the writings of tradition he adds, "What book of the holy, catholic Fathers does not echo this, so that we may reach our creator by a straight way?"[3] First is the quantitative difference: a "page or word" on the one hand, a "book" on the other. Secondly, there is the difference between "most straight" and merely "straight." Thirdly, the Scriptures are the primary source of guidance, the Fathers constitute an "echo." We will have to read more of the Fathers to extract their specific nourishment. And at times we will have to endure or skip over inevitable *longueurs*.

Secondly, we need initiation into the Fathers simply because without such background we will find ourselves floundering. There are more introductions available now than there were twenty years ago and there is an entire series entitled *Message of the Fathers of the Church*. These I will discuss in the next section. The problem with many of these is that the authors of these introductions are interested in the patristic writers from a historical or theological viewpoint. For us who look to the Fathers for *lectio divina*, something different may be needed. A knowledge of the times and contemporary church issues is certainly significant background, but perhaps there is an opening for an introduction to the Fathers that would see them primarily as practitioners and preachers of prayer, holiness, and gospel living.[4]

Even though, alongside the Scriptures, I have used the texts of tradition for *lectio* for more than twenty years, I know that there are difficulties involved. Some experience them more heavily than others. Those whose professional background is scientific or commercial, for instance, may never have developed a facility with literature that is on a par with their expertise in other areas. My experience has been that it is worthwhile persevering with the attempt. To facilitate this I will offer a few suggestions about how some problems can be eased.

Overcoming difficulties

In 1976 I wrote an article entitled, "Eleven Difficulties in Reading the Fathers."[5] Rereading the text eighteen years later, I am struck by the fact that today we are much better endowed with resources for patristic initiation than we were then.[6] In addition, Pope John Paul II wrote an Apostolic Letter on the sixteenth centenary of the death of Saint Basil of Caesarea,[7] and the Vatican Congregation for Catholic Education issued an *Instruction on the Study of the Fathers of the Church in the Formation of Priests* on November 10, 1989.[8] Some raising of consciousness has taken place in the last two decades.

If we are to arrive at the point of using the Fathers as *lectio*, we first need some foundational contact. What usually happens is that a potential reader comes across a text from a traditional writer, is attracted by it, and then seeks a greater exposure to this author. The initial contact can come about in a variety of ways: through general reading or from a biography, by references and quotations in spiritual books or by means of longer extracts in anthologies – for example, the *Philokalia* and the Office of Readings in the *Roman Breviary*.[9] It is this first attraction that arouses our interest; without it many of us would never venture into this hitherto unexplored territory.

The first problem we have is finding texts of the Fathers. The concluding parts of this chapter give some elementary indications on this point. After that we have to make a selection, since not everything the Fathers wrote is suitable for *lectio divina*. This may involve a little experimentation, trying a particular text and judging for yourself whether it is likely to lead you to prayerful reflection at this stage of your life.

When we begin reading the Fathers we become aware that there is a certain difference about the way they write. For many people difference means difficulty. Accordingly, let us examine some of the components of patristic writing that makes it unlike most modern spiritual books.

Translation. None of the ancient Fathers and comparatively few of the other traditional authors wrote in English. This means that we do not have direct contact with their thought. It comes to us filtered through the sensibility of a translator. Translators often have to make a choice between rendering the words exactly as they were written and conveying the feeling behind the words; in practice they usually decide in favor of a literal rendering. This means that priority is given to the logical content often at the expense of its emotional context. Often we end with a correct text, but one that is muffled and somehow lacking in humanity. This is the most obvious of the difficulties under which we labor. When the translation is in the style of the last century, we feel doubly excluded.

Language. The style of patristic writing is different than what is familiar to us from newspapers, novels, and lawn mower manuals. Like poetry, it is full of imagery and symbolism, and many people complain that it is "too flowery." Worse than that is the artificiality of so much of the allegory we find in the Fathers. There is no denying this. All I can say is that you become accustomed to it and learn either to enjoy it or to skip over it when it becomes too irksome.[10]

Thought progression. The logic of most of the Fathers is extremely fuzzy by our standards. Most of them thought, spoke, and argued in a right-brain mode, preferring imaginative allusion and intuition to the stolid reasonableness of logical sequence. We find their "proofs" unconvincing and less than watertight. They are not value-free, as we prefer, and presuppose in the reader what we are not prepared to take for granted. Here again we have to remind ourselves that the Fathers operated in a different world; we have to be prepared to make some concessions if we are to understand them.

Pastoral priorities. Since the Fathers were, almost by definition, pastors, most of what they composed had a pastoral purpose. Few of them took up the pen for amusement or for "intellectual" reasons. They did not write for the sake of writing, but as a reaction or response to circumstances. Their treatises and sermons were dictated to sustain their congregations in the concrete situations in which they found themselves. Even when they attacked a heretic, it was more to bolster the faithful than merely to refute the apostate. To us their preoccupations are often invisible. Because our needs are different, we sometimes miss their concerns. So the text seems to us drier than it need be. It is good to keep in mind that what we read was written to strengthen faith, to improve the quality of daily life, and to lead to prayer. That is why, once we reconstruct the context, such writings often serve us well for *lectio divina*.

Platonism. There are those who find the Hellenistic content of patristic writing unacceptable. In particular one hears of "platonic" dualism and the consequent negativity toward the world and the flesh. In a later section of this chapter, I will attempt to answer this criticism. For the moment it is sufficient to say that Hellenistic philosophy is an essential part of the culture of the patristic period. It cannot be ignored if we are to understand the Fathers. As we shall see, it also made a positive contribution to the development of spirituality – though, like every other philosophy, it had its limitations and errors.

Longueurs. It is true that occasionally one meets passages that are dull and boring and seem to lack any spiritual content. Sometimes it is a digression or an irrelevance to us; at other times it is too heavy with philosophy and theology to sustain our interest. These are all aspects of the otherness that is an essential part of contact with the authors of tradition. There is not a great deal to be done to ease our dissatisfaction; it is one of the negative elements in a practice that is, however, overwhelmingly positive. Sometimes we will need to skip over passages that try our patience; this is a survival skill necessary for long-term exposure to patristic thought.

I recognize that all these difficulties are real and have experienced them myself. Most of them belong to the intrinsic burden of reading the Fathers although they will be more intense for some readers and in connection with some Fathers. My main response to such objections is to say that the fruits of persevering with the Fathers outweigh the difficulties. I cannot prove that, but it has been my experience.

Perhaps the best way to build up a tolerance to these difficulties in communication is to become "emotionally involved" with one of the figures of the ancient Church. This may lead us to read a biography that will help the person come alive.[11] Reading letters is another way to become acquainted with someone.[12] From our central interest we then allow our enthusiasm to roam more widely until we build up some familiarity with the circle in which these various people moved and the world they inhabited. We do this not to become experts, but gradually to feel a little more at home in another century.

Monastic writers

If we are looking for writings with a more direct bearing on spirituality, we will often find this in the texts that derive from the monastic tradition. It would be a pity if we thought that these writings were only for monks and nuns – especially since the definition of "monastic" in those days was much broader than it is today. Sometimes in a sense it could include almost anyone who was seriously living a spiritual life. In addition, many of the great ecclesial figures such as Athanasius, Augustine, Basil, Chrysostom and Gregory the Great were closely associated with various forms of monastic living, and some of their writings reflect this.

To begin with, the *Sayings* of the great men and women of the desert are stimulating reading for almost anyone interested in the spiritual life. Short, pungent, anecdotal, and evangelical, they communicate new insights in a way impossible for learned treatises. Furthermore, they are not merely random reminiscences. They have been systematically preserved precisely for their usefulness to later generations. To track through the Fathers following the monastic trail is a good way to become habituated to using patristic texts as *lectio divina*. The place to start is with the Desert Fathers.

There are other writings that are but a step away from this primal experience: the works of Evagrius of Pontus, for instance, who tries to blend the scriptural and theological synthesis of Origen with the pragmatic and experiential tradition of the desert. John Cassian's *Conferences* were considered fundamental spiritual reading for at least a millennium after his death. The twenty-four reconstructed discourses offer a panorama of the whole field of spirituality; you will be surprised how apposite are many of his remarks. Basil the Great wrote rules for the urban communities living under his authority; simple, practical expositions built around scriptural texts and designed to foster evangelical living. His brother, Gregory of Nyssa, widower become monk become bishop, is among the foremost exponents of the theory and practice of contemplation. Saint Benedict of Nursia brought together many threads of earlier tradition to weave a pragmatic program of evangelical living that has been followed in the monasteries of the West ever since. Gregory the Great never forgot his monastic experience even when he became Pope; Scripture, the integrity of evangelical living, and contemplation are the themes to which he constantly returns in his preaching and writing. All this is a far cry from the barren polemics of theological controversy, and great grist for the mill of *lectio divina*.

In the second half of the first millennium the Latin tradition of spirituality was consolidated.[13] As it happened this was mainly the work of the monasteries. Monks and nuns of the benedictine tradition were characterized by two outstanding qualities: the love of learning and the desire for God.[14] They were serious about their spiritual lives and they were devoted to reading. Inevitably this resulted in an attachment to those elements of tradition that reflected their own spiritual experience. An informal canon of patristic writings developed. These were the books most often read in public and in private.[15] More important, these were the books copied and therefore most often available, even in small monastic libraries.[16] While being broad enough to escape the charge of ideology, this canon created sufficient cohesion and convergence to provide a foundation for further development.

Among the strongest factors in the development of Western spirituality was the formative power of the Latin liturgy. By it monastics were constantly exposed to the aural Bible in such a way that large slabs seemed to remain permanently in memory. The Fathers were also read daily and the liturgical texts were popularly linked with their names. The result of this was a common spiritual language that began to influence the way many authors wrote. Unconsciously their style echoed the cadences of the liturgy and, because of this, their writings found easy entrance into the minds and hearts of those similarly formed. The Bible, the liturgy, and the Fathers all sounded alike, so it is not surprising to find that preaching and teaching followed the lead. The monastic writers differ from the later exponents of Scholasticism because unaffectedly they speak the language of tradition.

The writers of the twelfth century deserve special attention. This was a very special period in history with some striking parallels to our own time and some significant differences.[17] On the one hand, there was great change in society and in the Church. A new humanism was developing in which concern for the person and interest in experience were paramount. On the other, it was still the age of faith, there was no break with tradition, and the dichotomy between reason and revelation was only just beginning. The spiritual literature generated at this time, especially by the first generations of Cistercians, managed to combine the traditional spirituality with contemporary humanism in a way that continues to have a strong impact. The solidity of fundamental doctrine is there, but it is filtered by centuries of spiritual experience and re-expressed in lyric language that adds a lightness of touch to the final product. The appeal to twentieth century people is such that a publishing house has been established with the purpose of propagating these works in a modern idiom, since there is clearly a market. Although much later than those who are strictly termed "Fathers of the Church," the monastic authors of the twelfth century continue to write in the patristic manner, but with the added asset of several centuries of insight and experience. This is perhaps why the learned seventeenth-century scholar Jean Mabillon termed Bernard of Clairvaux, "the last of the Fathers and surely not less than the first."[18]

An easy entry into the world of patristic thought is by this route. I frequently recommend the *Liturgical Sermons* of Guerric of Igny as a painless way of initiation into using the Fathers for *lectio divina*. There are several advantages in reading Guerric.

First, his is a very attractive personality. His approach to most subjects is moderate, gentle, and pastoral. As an older man he is wise, experienced, and mellow. He writes simply and competently and there is an air of peacefulness about his presentation. Depth of feeling and poetic imagination combine to bring the reader to a different space.

Secondly, his sermons are linked with the liturgical year. It is possible to read one or several as the liturgical seasons go by – as a means of reflecting on Advent or Lent, for example. In this way, this part of our *lectio divina* prepares us for the celebration of the liturgy and interacts with its scriptural readings.

Another advantage of Guerric's sermons is that they are relatively short and self-contained. This means that we can read one or other of them as occasion warrants without having to commit ourselves to the whole series. Finally, the writings of Guerric are very much Bible-centered. They become for us a means of appreciating some hitherto unnoticed aspects of the scriptural text. In fact, reading the text of the *Liturgical Sermons* with the Bible open alongside is a very profitable way of finding prayer.

If we enjoy Guerric we may feel drawn to try some of the other writings of the Cistercian Fathers. Each has his own special quality. Bernard of Clairvaux is a brilliant writer with keen insights into the deep matters of spirituality and a firm grasp of human realities. In his lifetime Aelred of Rievaulx was renowned for his amiability and he writes well of love in his treatises *The Mirror of Charity* and *Spiritual Friendship*. William of St. Thierry displayed a great power for introspection and a mastery of theology. The Englishmen John of Forde and Gilbert of Swineshead have much to say about contemplation. And there are many more. These are the writers that had a profound effect on the spiritual formation of Thomas Merton.[19] The end product of his reading them was not an antiquarian spirituality, but a firm spiritual stance that was capable of entering into dialogue with the modern world. So it can be with us.

After many years of faithfully reading the Bible, we may find that our understanding is enhanced by using some of our *lectio* time in reading such Fathers. One of the advantages of the exercise is that they can take us back to the Scriptures by a different route so that we begin to perceive in the sacred text elements of which we had previously been unaware. The writings of tradition never replace the Scriptures. What they do is to broaden the base of our biblical understanding and somehow make the Scriptures more fresh and alive.

The spirituality of the Fathers

The writers of tradition are many and their philosophies varied. Any general survey of their spiritual doctrine may seem jejune. There is, however, one way of approaching the matter that may lead us to significant conclusions. The end of the patristic era of theology coincided with the adoption of Aristotelian thought in the West. What unites the Fathers is that they belonged to what may be loosely termed a "platonizing" sphere of influence.[20]

Plato was a Greek philosopher of the fourth century before Christ. His thought is contained in a dozen or so dialogues in which fundamental ethical and metaphysical issues are discussed. His doctrines continued after his death. Their contact with Judaism is signalled by the book of Wisdom and in the writings of Philo of Alexandria, a contemporary of Christ. A new synthesis was achieved in the third century A.D. by Plotinus that is termed Neoplatonism.

Aristotle followed Plato but adopted a completely different approach to that of his master. Where Plato was intuitive, poetic, synthetic, and circular in his presentation (we would say right-brain), Aristotle was determinedly left-brain: analytic, organized, logical, empirical. Plato concerned himself with the totality, Aristotle concentrated on individual objects. In the celebrated painting by Raphael, *The School of Athens*, Plato points up to heaven, Aristotle gestures towards the earth. In general, Aristotle was not much esteemed by the Fathers, except as an empirical scientist; by many he was regarded as an atheist. Apart from considerable impact on Boetius in the sixth century, Aristotle did not begin to influence theological thought until the twelfth century when Jewish and Moslem translators and commentators reintroduced him to the West.

With Aristotelian thought there was no continuity between theological tradition and philosophy. The introduction of Aristotle drove a wedge between the two disciplines.[21] The situation was different with Platonism. Those who had been formed in Platonic categories used their previous training to formulate a language suitable for specifically Christian doctrine. Platonic thought played an integral role in the emergence and development of Christian theology.

This is not necessarily something to be regretted. Christianity was born into a Hellenistic world. Just as its expansion was aided by the means of communication provided by the Roman Empire, so its deepening was facilitated by the wisdom tradition of ancient Greece. It is hard to imagine the theology of Paul or the Gospel of John without some Hellenistic background. The existence of Platonic thought is part of the facticity of the Incarnation.

Here we are not speaking about a literary dependence of Christian texts on Platonic exemplars. Platonism was never a strict system in the way that Aristotelianism was. It worked with totalities and there was a lot of fuzziness and overlap when it came to details. Inevitably, Stoic and Pythagorean influences changed the content of some ideas and there was development within Platonism itself. This is why I use the expression "platonizing." In its influence on Christian thought, Platonism was more a tendency than an overt school of thought.

There is a central truth in Platonism that found a ready welcome in Christian thinkers. Beyond that there are other themes that develop its practical implications. Later spirituality was to draw on many of these as well. The process was not uncritical. Only what was considered to concord with the Gospel was accepted, and even then it was filtered through the Christian sensibility of many generations. In a certain sense it could be said that Platonism was baptized and only thus was it allowed to contribute to the evolution of Christian theological thought.

Plato assigned a higher priority to the spiritual world than to the complex of material events that make up our mundane existence. Thus he introduced the dilemma that is at the heart of many religious traditions: the dialectic between reality and appearances. Popular critics today criticize Plato for "not taking the world seriously." This is a misreading of the texts. What is being said is that the world of sense and common experience has no intrinsic and autonomous meaning; its meaning depends on its relationship to an unseen world that is not subject to its limitations. Christians read this as saying that without God all that we know is absurd. The true meaning of life is not immediately accessible, but has to be sought in transcendence. Thus the word "invisible" in the Nicene Creed was not considered a liability, but a necessary consequence of God's spiritual nature. This is no more than we find affirmed in the New Testament: "We look not to what is seen but to what is unseen. What is seen is transient; what is unseen is eternal" (2 Corinthians 4:18).

The alliance of Christian thought with Platonism depends on this fundamental assertion that human life makes sense only when it is viewed in relationship with an ultimate and transcendent reality. That is the point of convergence. The fact that Christians depart from Plato in identifying this ultimate reality with the God of Israel as revealed in Jesus does not alter their profound agreement that human beings are called to "seek what is above" (Colossians 3:1) and to expect no lasting contentment from material existence. "If for this life only we have hope in Christ, then of all human beings we are those who are to be pitied most" (1 Corinthians 15:19). Platonism, however imperfect and erroneous in itself, was seen as a defense against prevailing materialism. Both Justin the Apologist and Saint Augustine later realized that "conversion" to Platonism was a preliminary step in the direction of Christianity.

Building upon this fundamental tenet, various subsidiary themes developed in which the fusion of horizons was extended. Let us look at some of the more important emphases in which patristic spirituality was enriched by the experience and reflection of platonizing philosophy.

Image and likeness. Because spirituality is a reflection on the relationship between the human being and God, it demands not only a knowledge of God (theology) but also an understanding of human reality (anthropology). A characteristic of patristic spirituality is the detailed attention given to anthropological issues. This is especially true of Augustine, Gregory of Nyssa, and the Cistercian Fathers.[22] The favored means of affirming the basic compatibility of human and divine, and the consequent vocation of humans to become more divine, was by reference to the theme of image and likeness. The basis for the theme is found in Genesis 1:26–27, but much of the content of its elucidation came from the accumulated fund of philosophic reflection. The vocabulary used by the Fathers was similar to that current in philosophic circles. In addition, following Saint Paul's difficulty in preaching resurrection to Hellenists (Acts 17), the Fathers were happy to borrow from Plato the notion of the inherent immortality of the human soul. There are differences, of course, but the area of overlap remains considerable.

Memory. Many readers of Augustine's *Confessions* have been puzzled by the attention he gives to this topic. The idea of memory both as faculty and act of perception is important in the Platonic tradition. Like many Christian writers, Augustine accepted the division of the soul into reason or intellect, memory, and will, but his approach to memory is original. While progressively distancing his conclusions from the notion of the pre-existence of souls, he still affirmed, in contrast to Aristotle, that the memory gave access to realities not attainable by the senses. From the doctrine of the human being as the image of God, a certain affinity of nature was affirmed: human and divine are not incompatible. The "memory" is this ontological divine residue in the center of personal existence. Thus, the *memoria* was seen as the doorway to the spiritual world. God is to be sought and found in the memory, even though, in another sense, God is beyond the actual content of remembering.

The metaphysical notion of memory thus combines with the theme of mindfulness. We must consciously and voluntarily cultivate the active memory of God as a means of realizing our own inherent divine potential. We know that the theme of remembering is constant in the book of Deuteronomy and in Wisdom literature; this theme fed into the platonizing stream to result in an enduring emphasis in Christian spirituality on the memory of God: *memoria Dei*.[23] It is a favorite motif among Cistercian writers, attested to by the popular hymn *Jesu dulcis memoria*: "Jesus, the Very Thought of Thee."[24]

Self-knowledge. The injunction of the Delphic oracle, "Know yourself," was widely accepted in both Greek philosophy and Christian spirituality. Originally this axiom was intended as a reminder of human mortality, then later its sense was expanded to the ethical sphere. Live in accordance with what you are! Forgetfulness was seen as the major cause of alienation from God, and so a return to God begins when, like the Prodigal Son, we turn back to ourselves. Spiritual life coincides with the ascent to truth and the progressive putting aside of delusion and false identity.

Interiority. Self-knowledge requires that we cease taking our definition of self from exterior factors alone, as though we were mere figments of material and social processes, and instead look to our inner status. The true philosopher and the Christian alike are required to give priority to inward realities such as conscience, memory, and freedom of choice. This may entail a certain refusal of demands emanating from outside – a certain resistance to the world and the senses. Leo the Great constantly calls on Christians to recognize their "dignity." No matter what our outward status, we are free; it is the recognition of this liberated condition that must govern all practical choices. Perhaps the *homo interior* of Romans 7:22 is an echo of a phrase in Plato's *Republic* (Book 9,589).

Purification. Self-awareness brings a realization that there is a struggle between our freedom and those realities that enslave us, be they purely external, or what we have internalized in the past, or even "daimonic" (we would probably name them "unconscious"). When we are alerted to opposed principles within, we are brought to the point of making a choice about which influences will shape the course of our life. This means encouraging some tendencies and inhibiting others. Pleasure is not a good guide to what is creative. As a result we will often have to abstain from what is gratifying or commit ourselves to what is laborious in order to satisfy our inner demands.

Thus, there is a role for the negative elements of discipleship: abstinence and asceticism. This means subjecting our emotions or passions to discernment and compelling those that are unruly (the vices) to accept the governance of the will under grace. Consistent practice gradually cleanses our system of its poisons and leads to that purity of heart which, according to the Beatitudes, sees God. When the Fathers and the philosophers spoke about *apatheia* (or victory over the passions) they were more interested in the single-heartedness that was its effect than in mere denial or suppression of instinctual impulses.[25] As Peter Brown has noted, the ascetical movement was not a denial of the body but an affirmation of its importance; instead of dismissing bodily impulses as insignificant to the state of the soul, it affirmed the interdependence of the state of the passions and the operation of the spirit.[26] *Katharsis* or purification was a necessary process in realizing the potential inherent in the spiritual nature of human beings.

Ascent by degrees. From the second century A.D., platonizing philosophy propagated the view of a gradated universe of beings. Between ultimate reality and matter, a role was assigned to intermediary spirits. This obviously contributed to Christian teaching about angels and devils and their role in protecting or undermining our commitment. It also provided an image for spiritual growth. Human beings are suspended halfway between ultimate spiritual reality and its material counter-principle. The work of asceticism or purification is to move away from the material fragmentation towards the harmony and unity of the spiritual world. This ascent provides the measure of spiritual growth. The closer we come to God, the more we share in the divine attributes.

Participation. In the Platonic view, lower forms exist by virtue of their participation in what is highest. Being flows downward. Ultimate reality communicates its nature to lower beings.[27] Skirting the philosophical problems inherent in the strict logic of this theory, the Fathers eagerly seized on the idea of participation as an explanation of spirituality; we have become "sharers in the divine nature" (2 Peter 1:4). There is a commonality of nature between us and God, "in whom we live and move and have our being" (Acts 17:28). Viewed from this angle, human spiritual perfection consists in attaching ourselves more fully to the source of our being and, therefore, progressively detaching ourselves from "lower" principles of activity.

Moving from a philosophical perspective to mysticism, the concept of participation offers an explanation of contemplative experience. By setting aside all that constitutes our own subjectivity, we enter into the subjectivity of Christ. We are silent, it is Christ who prays within us. Our awareness of God is not that generated by our previous spiritual history and recycled. It is "seeing" the Father through the eyes of Christ, sharing the Spirit, and consenting to be lifted beyond our limited capacities. We are "in Christ" by participation.

Desire for God. Intelligent beings, aware of their nature and destiny, understand that without participation in the life of God their existence is incomplete. Perhaps particular events reinforce this sense of deprivation. And so develops a yearning for the completion that comes when God will become "all in all" (1 Corinthians 15:28). If the human being is created capable of union with God, then we experience frustration when this potentiality is denied. To the extent that this frustration derives from our status as pilgrims, Christians are aware of a nostalgia for the heavenly homeland that makes them cry out, "Here we have no abiding city" (Hebrews 13:14). The image of the Fall and banishment is as strong in Platonism as it is among readers of Genesis; some blending of themes was inevitable. "Our citizenship is in heaven" (Philippians 3:20); why be surprised if we feel alienated when we are "away from the Lord" (2 Corinthians 5:6)? Acceptable as such a sentiment might be to a confirmed Platonist, its immediate source is New Testament experience, not philosophy.[28]

Contemplation. Contemplation had a high priority in the

Platonic tradition. It was regarded as the supremely human activity – that by which we become fully alive and fully ourselves. This priority was accepted almost without question by most of the Fathers. The ultimate flowering of contemplation would occur in heaven. Eternal joy was seen as the result of seeing God (the "beatific vision").

At one level, the word "contemplation" refers simply to the act of seeing. Yet it has an intensity about it that lifts it above our ordinary experience of vision. The contemplative state has a certain intensity. It includes an absorption in the object, a total concentration that makes one inattentive to anything else. This is why the term is inappropriately used of objects that cannot sustain our total attention. It describes well what occurs in those who serve God with undivided hearts. The measure of such contemplation is the degree of conformity between us and God. The experience becomes stronger as our will is more fully and firmly conjoined to God's will. In other words, contemplation is the ultimate fruit of the "obedience of faith." When all rebellion disappears in us, and opportunity presents itself, the experience of prayer becomes an experience of union even to the point where the mystics speak of "fusion" or "identification" with God. Listen to Plotinus speak of this:

> There were not two; beholder was one with beheld; it was not a vision compassed but a unity apprehended. The man formed by this mingling with the Supreme must – if he only remember – carry its image impressed upon him: he is become the Unity, nothing within him or without inducing any diversity; no movement now, no passion, no outlooking desire, once this ascent is achieved; reasoning is in abeyance and all Intellection and even, to dare the word, the very self; caught away, filled with God, he has in perfect stillness attained isolation; all the being calmed, he turns neither to this side nor to that, not even inwards to himself; utterly resting he has become very rest. He belongs no longer to the order of the beautiful; he has risen above beauty; he has over passed even the choir of the virtues; he is like one who, having penetrated the inner sanctuary, leaves the temple images behind him – though these become once more first objects of regard when he leaves the holies; for There his converse was not with image, not with trace, but with the very Truth in the view of which all the rest is but secondary.[29]

This is not much different from the language that Christian

mystics made their own to describe the reality of their spiritual experience.[30]

Spiritual marriage. Perhaps the most potent symbol of contemplative experience is that of spiritual marriage. Here again, there is a convergence of Christian and platonizing language. In his *Symposium* (Book 10, 389), Plato speaks of the marriage of the soul with subsistent Beauty and the birth of the virtues as resulting from this union. Philo of Alexandria and the Gnostics contributed to the theme and it became commonplace among the Fathers, first to describe the union of Christ and the Church (as in Ephesians 5:23–33) and then that between individuals and God. As in other areas discussed, we may have here a case of convergence of language rather than literary dependence; the fact remains that the similarity is striking.

Illumination. Similarly, the appropriation of the imagery of light and darkness served as a bridge between Christian and Platonic thought. Plato and Plotinus on one side, Clement of Alexandria, Augustine, and Gregory of Nyssa on the other, were all great exponents of the struggle of the human spirit to evade the darkness of selfish passion and be filled with the divine light. Any moment of transition from death to life, from old to new, from ignorance to understanding thus qualified as enlightenment. For the early Christians, for example, this was also the term used for baptism. It remains a good image of what we experience throughout life as grace takes hold of us.

Divinization. Sharers in the divine nature, we are called to become ever more possessed by the fullness of God. Christian life is not being good but becoming God. Plato himself did not speak about divinization, but referred to the innate affinity or kinship between human and divine. Contemplation has the effect of increasing the likeness to the divine within us and brings to realization our initial potential.[31] The theme was more explicitly stated in later philosophy and in the Fathers from the time of Ignatius of Antioch and Clement of Alexandria.[32] Divinization is a very strong emphasis in the Greek Fathers and, from the fifth century, it was important in Latin theology, although it tended to be displaced by other themes such as redemption, the theology of the Church as mystical body of Christ, and the notion of grace. Divinization experienced a revival in the West in the monastic writers of the eleventh and twelfth centuries such as Anselm of Canterbury and the Cistercians. It also recurs in the Rhenish and Flemish mystics of the fourteenth century.

These themes I sketch in paltry detail. They represent some of the valuable contributions made by platonizing philosophy to the development of Christian spirituality. There are liabilities involved in these concepts, if interpreted grossly or out of context. In the Fathers, however, such notions were accepted not because they were current, but because they offered a coherent explanation of what they themselves had experienced. Taken collectively, and availing ourselves of the filtering process that the Fathers themselves applied, these themes give an excellent account of what happens in the spiritual life. We can certainly learn something from them.

An impressionistic survey of the literature

In this section I am going to take you on a quick tour of the whole area of patristic writings. What I point out is necessarily subjective and eclectic. It will reflect my own journey and experience and doubtless reveal something of the extent of my ignorance. I am not suggesting that you read everything, as I have not, but simply that you know it exists.

It is an education to visit a good patristic library. The texts themselves (with some duplication) fill the best part of 1,000 encyclopedia-size volumes. Long the standard reference for Latin and Greek Fathers was the work of J. P. Migne published in the period 1844–66: 222 volumes of *Patrologia Latina* (= *PL*) and 168 volumes of *Patrologia Graeca* (= *PG*). More recent, more critical, and more expensive editions are found in over 200 volumes in the different series of *Corpus Christianorum* (= *CChr*), published by the Belgian publisher Brepols. Other collections include *Corpus Scriptorum Ecclesiasticorum Latinorum* (= *CSEL*) from Vienna and the Berlin Corpus of Greek Fathers (= *GCS*). Syriac and Oriental (including Coptic and Slavonic) collections are also available. The French have produced bilingual editions with good notes and introductions for about 400 works in the *Sources Chrétiennes* (= *SChr*) series. The lesson we learn is one of humility. There is more here than anyone will ever read in a lifetime, much less master.

It is a relief to pass from ancient languages to English. At least we can understand the words! Apart from individual translations and studies, there are several series.

- *Ante-Nicene Fathers*. This series was begun in 1866 by T. Clark, the Lord Provost of Edinburgh, who was also a publisher and an Elder of the Free Church of Scotland. The original twenty-four volumes were reduced to eight for the American edition and an index volume and a supplement were added. (= ANF)

- *Nicene and Post-Nicene Fathers*. These volumes were begun under the initiative of the founders of the Oxford Movement in 1837 with a special concentration on exegetical works. In 1886 the forty-eight original volumes were republished in the United States in twenty-eight volumes. Eight volumes are devoted to Augustine and six to Chrysostom: the other Fathers are spread through the remaining fourteen. (= NPNF)

Both sets have been reprinted in uniform format by Eerdmans and are relatively inexpensive.[33] Their chief value is that they make it possible for those without Latin and Greek to verify references. The translations are cumbersome with many complex sentences. At times the rendering is theologically tendentious and some texts have been bowdlerized to conform with nineteenth century sensibilities.[34] I have known some who have used them for personal reading, but I would not recommend it if a better version is available. For beginners a clearer page and a more contemporary style are probably advisable.

- *The Fathers of the Church*. This series of patristic (and more recently medieval) translations has been sponsored for more than half a century by the Catholic University of America. They are attractive books and the translations are clear and accurate. A limited amount of introductory and explanatory material is included. The series is suitable for reflective reading, although not all titles are relevant. (= FC)

- *Ancient Christian Writers*. Originally published by the Newman Press (Longmans in Britain) and now issued by the Paulist Press, these volumes are clear and up-to-date and make good reading. They are usually well-equipped with notes. A 1992 volume on Irenaeus (ACW 55) has eighteen pages of introduction, eighty-four pages of text, 165 pages of notes, and twenty-seven pages of indices. (= ACW)

- *Classics of Western Spirituality*. The scope of this series produced by the Paulist Press is very wide, but it contains many significant works of the Christian spiritual tradition. It shares with the previous two series the advantages of being clear, contemporary and attractive to read. It is available in both hardcover and paperback format. (= CWS)

• *The Library of Christian Classics.* This is a twenty-six volume set from the Westminster Press in Philadelphia that includes not only the Fathers but also later authors. Its Ichthus Edition is paperback. (= LCC)

• *Cistercian Fathers Series.* This is published by Cistercian Publications, associated with Western Michigan University in Kalamazoo. There is a companion series *Cistercian Studies Series* which includes texts from the broader monastic tradition and studies. Together the two series number more than 200 volumes. Although the quality of translation is uneven, the series is valuable because most of the texts were originally written with a view to *lectio divina*. There are paperback editions of some titles. (= Cistercian)

• *Penguin Classics.* A browse through the wide world of Penguin Classics will reveal several titles from Christian tradition. This can be an inexpensive way to begin a personal library of major works from the Christian tradition. (= Penguin)

In many cases there are several translations of a single work available in different series and there may be others published separately. It is important to find a version written in contemporary English. I always pay more attention to the copyright date than to the glossy cover; it has been known that old translations are republished as though they were recent. Editions with good introductions and notes can contribute much to an intelligent reading and deserve preference when other factors are equal.

Beyond the texts themselves, there are many books that offer us an insight into the patristic world and give guidance about how we can best approach it. Here are some titles that I have stumbled across.

• Adalbert Hamman, *How to Read the Church Fathers*, Crossroad, New York, 1993. This is a large-format book with definitions, maps, tables, pictures, and extracts from the Fathers. It is a book for browsing, but probably the first title I would recommend to most people starting a patristic adventure.

• Boniface Ramsey, *Beginning to Read the Fathers*, Paulist Press, New York, 1985. Mainly an introduction to the patristic world of thought and concern, but with a reading program, select bibliography, and chronology.

• Maurice Wiles, *The Christian Fathers*, Oxford University Press, New York, 1982 and Aelred Squire, *Asking the Fathers*, Morehouse-Barlow, New York, 1973 cover patristic themes and impressions.

• Aelred Squire, *Fathers Talking: An Anthology*, Cistercian Publications (CS 93), Kalamazoo, 1986 reproduces extracts of one or two pages or more.

• Donald W. Wuerl, *Fathers of the Church*, Our Sunday Visitor, Huntington, 1975 gives short popular biographies of sixteen Fathers.

• C. Mondésert, *Pour lire les Pères de l'Église: dans la collection "Sources Chrétiennes,"* Cerf, Paris, 1979. This gives a bird's-eye view of the more than 300 titles in the *Sources Chrétiennes* series, with maps, chronologies, and useful summaries.

• Thomas Halton (General Editor), *Message of the Fathers of the Church* (twenty-two volumes projected), Michael Glazier, Wilmington. A series of volumes by different authors on various themes including prayer, moral teaching, ministry, and social thought.

• Oliver Davies (Series Editor), *The Spirituality of the Fathers*. Four brief volumes have appeared so far from New City, London.

• M. F. Toal (trans.), *Patristic Homilies on the Gospels: The Sunday Sermons of the Great Fathers* (four volumes), Longmans Green, London, from 1954. These are older books and are tailored to suit the pre-Vatican II lectionary, but contain a wealth of sermon material not otherwise easy to procure in translation. Usually the texts read easily, though critical editions were not always available and sometimes the translator took short cuts.

• To this list could be added many books that describe the life of the Church in the first centuries. From the excellent presentations available, two titles that are inexpensive and particularly good as introductions to patristic reading are Henry Chadwick, *The Early Church* (The Pelican History of the Church, 1), Penguin Viking, New York, 1993 and Patrick Verbraken, *The Beginnings of the Church: The First Christian Centuries*, Paulist Press, New York, 1968.

These are general titles. It is not possible in a book such as this to give a detailed listing of the many hundreds of studies, surveys, and biographies that cast light on the patristic period and those who inhabit it. Nobody will read them all, and those who become interested in this area are generally more guided by availability and their own attractions than by any "objective" listing. I tend to think that it is better to move on to the writings of the Fathers themselves, than to spend too much time reading about them. In any case, introductions are often more appreciated when we have questions and difficulties from our reading that need to be addressed.

A personal reading list

Whenever I speak about reading the Fathers as *lectio divina* I am asked to provide a list of suitable works. What follows is a response to that request. The titles listed begin with the second century and stretch into the fourteenth. I have limited myself to what I have personally read and to what is available in English. When I know of translations published in any of the series mentioned in the previous section, I indicate this. The listing is approximately chronological.

Anonymous, *The Didache*, ACW, Penguin.

Ignatius of Antioch, *Letters*, ANF, ACW, Penguin.

Desert Fathers, *Sayings*, Cistercian.

Evagrius of Pontus, *Chapters on Prayer*, Cistercian.

Origen, *On Prayer*, LCC, CWS.

Cyprian of Carthage, *The Good of Patience*, *On the Lord's Prayer*, FC.

Athanasius of Alexandria, *Life of Antony*, ACW, CWS; *Letter to Marcellinus*, CWS.

Basil the Great, *Short and Long Rules*, FC.

Gregory of Nyssa, *On the Beatitudes*, ACW; *The Life of Moses*, CWS.

John Chrysostom, *Homilies on St. Matthew's Gospel*, NPNF; *Homilies on St. John's Gospel*, NPNF, FC.

Augustine of Hippo, *Confessions*, various; *On the Gospel of St. John*, NPNF; *On the First Epistle of St. John*, *On the Psalms*, NPNF, ACW; *Sermons*.

John Cassian, *Conferences*, NPNF, CWS, LCC.

Patrick, *Confession*, ACW.

Leo the Great, *Sermons*, NPNF.

Gregory the Great, *Homilies on the Gospels*, Cistercian.

Caesarius of Arles, *Sermons*, FC.

Dorotheos of Gaza, *Discourses*, Cistercian.

Guigo II, *The Ladder of Monks*, Cistercian.

William of St.Thierry, *Golden Epistle*, Cistercian.

Bernard of Clairvaux, *On the Necessity of Loving God*, Cistercian, CWS; *Sermons on the Song of Songs*, Cistercian.

Beatrice of Nazareth, *The Seven Modes of Love*, Cistercian.

Guerric of Igny, *Liturgical Sermons*, Cistercian.

Aelred of Rievaulx, *The Mirror of Charity*, *Spiritual Friendship*, Cistercian.

Gertrude of Helfta, *Exercises*, Cistercian.

Anonymous, *The Cloud of Unknowing*, CWS.

Julian of Norwich, *Revelations of Divine Love*, CWS.

APPENDIX

Patristic authors in the Roman Breviary

Here is a statistical breakdown of the frequency of the major patristic authors in the Roman Breviary; it gives some idea of their relative importance in the liturgical tradition of the Western Church. Some figures are inflated because a particular work is read continuously over the space of a week. The Fathers most often read are in **bold type**. By way of comparison, the frequency with which each Father is cited in *The Catechism of the Catholic Church* is indicated in parentheses. The main difference is the lower proportion of monastic authors.

Aelred of Rievaulx	3	(–)
Ambrose of Milan	**25**	(21)
Athanasius of Alexandria	11	(3)
Augustine of Hippo	**80**	(87)
Baldwin of Ford	4	(–)
Basil of Caesarea	8	(7)
Bede the Venerable	5	(–)
Bernard of Clairvaux	16	(2)
Caesarius of Arles	3	(1)
Clement of Alexandria	10	(1)
Clement of Rome	13	(5)
Columbanus of Bobbio	5	(–)
Cyprian of Carthage	**19**	(11)
Cyril of Jerusalem	9	(7)
Ephrem the Syrian	5	(–)
Fulgentius of Ruspe	7	(1)
Gregory the Great	19	(6)

Gregory Nazianzen	7	(11)
Gregory of Nyssa	12	(10)
Hilary of Poitiers	7	(1)
Ignatius of Antioch	15	(16)
Irenaeus of Lyon	14	(32)
Isaac of Stella	4	(–)
Jerome	4	(3)
John Chrysostom	**20**	(18)
Justin Martyr	3	(9)
Leo the Great	**25**	(11)
Maximus the Confessor	4	(3)
Origen of Alexandria	8	(9)
Peter Chrysologus	7	(4)
Peter Damian	3	(–)
Polycarp	5	(3)
Tertullian	2	(14)
William of St. Thierry	2	(–)

NOTES

Abbreviations

ANF	*Ante-Nicene Fathers*, William B. Eerdmans, Grand Rapids, 1975.
CChr	*Corpus Christianorum*, Series Latina, Brepols, Turnhout, 1954–.
CS	Cistercian Studies Series, Cistercian Publications, Kalamazoo, 1970–.
CSQ	*Cistercian Studies Quarterly*
CWS	*Classics of Western Spirituality*, Paulist Press, New York, 1978–.
DSp	*Dictionnaire de Spiritualité*, Beauchesne, Paris, 1937–94.
FC	Fathers of the Church Series, Catholic University of America Press, 1947–.
NPNF	*Nicene and Post-Nicene Fathers*, William B. Eerdmans, Grand Rapids, 1952–56.
PG	*Patrologia Graeca* (ed.) J. P. Migne, Éditions Garnier, Paris, 1857–66.
PL	*Patrologia Latina* (ed.) J. P. Migne, Éditions Garnier, Paris, 1844–55.
RB	*Rule of St. Benedict*. Various editions and translations available.
SBO	*Sancti Bernardi Opera,* Editions Cistercienses, Rome, *1957—).*
SChr	*Sources Chrétiennes*, Cerf, Paris, 1942–.
Tjurunga	*Tjurunga: An Australasian Benedictine Review.*

Preface

1. When I use "benedictine" without a capital letter I am speaking broadly. I am not only referring to Benedictines, but to all those religious orders and lay associations that are animated by the Rule of Benedict and take their identity from the tradition of Western monastic spirituality.
2. Dom Columba Marmion (1858–1923) was an Irish diocesan priest who became a monk and later abbot of Maredsous in Belgium. His principal works, *Christ, the Life of the Soul*, *Christ in His Mysteries*, and *Christ, the Ideal of the Monk*, continued to be reprinted right up to the 1960s. If they have ceased to be popular it is probably because the language seems outdated today. Many also find difficulty in the abundant Latin quotations scattered through every page.
3. In monastic circles *lectio* is usually pronounced *léksio*.
4. I make an exception for García M. Colombás, *La lectura de Dios: approximación a la lectio divina*, Ediciones Monte Casino, Zamora, 1980.

Chapter 1

1. The priorities evident in early Cîteaux are clear from the primitive documents. From its foundation on March 21, 1098 until Christmas 1111, three major copying projects were undertaken: first the texts needed for the celebration of the liturgy, second the Bible, and third the *Moralia* of Saint Gregory the Great, comprising twenty-four books. The core collections of the monasteries up until the fourteenth century will reflect the same composition: liturgy, Scripture and patristics.
2. Initially, for the sake of simplicity of presentation, I am going to restrict the matter of *lectio divina* to the biblical books. As our discussion proceeds I will broaden the scope of *lectio* to include liturgical and ecclesial texts and the classical writings of Christian tradition. The rationale for this approach will become evident later on.
3. *RB* 48–49.
4. Whether we should be attempting to develop techniques of "audio divina" and "video divina" to meet the needs of a post-literate age is a question that is beyond the scope of this book and the competence of its author.
5. See, for example, Allan Bloom, *The Closing of the American Mind*, Simon & Schuster, New York, 1987, pp. 65–66.
6. See Benedicta Ward (trans.), *The Sayings of the Desert Fathers: The Alphabetical Collection* (CS 59), Cistercian Publications, Kalamazoo, 1975, p. 183, 162.
7. The standard division of the Bible into chapters seems to derive from Stephen Langton (d. 1228). The system of versification appeared in Robert Estienne's printed edition of the New Testament in 1551. Before this time different usages prevailed, and reference was often made by allusion to the content, presuming on the knowledge of the reader.
8. Deborah Tanner describes the "meta-message" in terms of information about the *relationship* existing among those involved in a conversation and their attitudes. See *You Just Don't Understand: Men and Women in Conversation*, Ballantine Books, New York, 1990, p. 32.
9. William of St. Thierry, *The Golden Epistle*, # 121; *SChr* 223, p. 238.
10. *RB* 48.17; see also *RB* 43.8.
11. I have written a brief description of acedia in Michael Downey (ed.), *The New Dictionary of Catholic Spirituality*, The Liturgical Press, Collegeville, 1993, pp. 4–5. Perhaps acedia relates to what is currently termed Attention Deficit Disorder.
12. Cardinal Newman explains this succinctly: "God has made us feel in order that we may *go on to act* in consequence of feeling; if then we allow our

feelings to be excited without acting upon them, we do mischief to the moral system within us, just as we might spoil a watch or other piece of mechanism, by playing with the wheels of it. We weaken its springs, and they cease to act truly. Accordingly, when we have got into the habit of amusing ourselves with these works of fiction, we come at length to feel the excitement without the slightest thought or tendency to act upon it ..." J. H. Newman, *Parochial and Plain Sermons*, Vol. II, Longmans, Green & Company, London, 1891, pp. 371–372. As Rollo May reminded us, the final result of overstimulation is loss of feeling. See *Love and Will*, Fontana, London, 1972, pp. 31–32.

13. Thomas Merton was fierce and extreme on this point. "The life of the television-watcher is a kind of caricature of contemplation. Passivity, uncritical absorption, receptivity, inertia. Not only that, but a gradual, progressive yielding to the mystic attraction until one is spellbound in a state of complete union. The trouble with this caricature is that it is really the exact opposite of contemplation ... [Contemplation] is the summit of a life of spiritual freedom. The other, the ersatz, is the nadir of intellectual and emotional slavery." "Inner Experience: Problems of the Contemplative Life (VII)," *CSQ* 19 (1984), pp. 269–270.

14. Dom Roger Hudleston (ed.), *The Spiritual Letters of Dom John Chapman O.S.B.*, Sheed & Ward, London, 1935, Letter 12, p. 53. An unsourced quotation from the correspondence of Gustave Flaubert makes the point that moments of creativity are often dependent on the matrix of a monotonous life: "Be boring and regular in your life, like a bourgeois, so that you can be violent and original in your work."

15. *Parochial and Plain Sermons*, Volume I, Rivingtons, London, 1873, Sermon 19: Times of Private Prayer.

16. *RB* 48.2.

17. #120; *SChr* 223, p. 238.

18. Thomas Merton, "Inner Experience: Problems of the Contemplative Life (VII)," *CSQ* 19 (1984), pp. 279–280.

19. See *RB* 20, "Reverence in Prayer."

20. *RB* 6.6.

21. #122; *SChr* 223, p. 240.

22. Sermon 300.2 among the sermons of Saint Augustine, *PL* 39, 2319c.

23. I have written about this in *Toward God: The Ancient Art of Western Prayer, Triumph, Liguori, MO, 1996*; pp. 43–45. For a more technical treatment see my *Athirst for God: Spiritual Desire in Bernard of Clairvaux's Sermons on the Song of Songs* (CS 77), Cistercian Publications, Kalamazoo, 1988, pp. 120–129.

24. Saint Athanasius of Alexandria, *Letter to Marcellinus*, 12; translated, for example, by R. Gregg in the *CWS* series, Paulist Press, New York, 1980, p. 111.

25. *RB* 28.3: *medicamina scripturarum divinarum.*

Chapter 2

1. Armand Veilleux, "Holy Scripture in the Pachomian Koinonia," *Monastic Studies* 10 (1974), pp. 143–153. More recently, Douglas Burton-Christie has written, "The increased attention that has been given to early monasticism in contemporary scholarship has contributed to a better understanding of the place of Scripture within early monasticism and of the particular culture which developed within that world." *The Word in the Desert: Scripture and the Quest for Holiness in Early Christian Monasticism*, Oxford University Press, New York, 1993, p. 15. The assertion is substantiated by a bibliography on pp. 29–30.

2. *RB* Prologue 50.

3. "Christ is the power of God and God's wisdom; one who does not know the Scriptures does not know God's power and wisdom. One who is ignorant of the Scriptures is ignorant of Christ." *In Isaiam prophetam*, Prologus 1–2; *PL* 24, col. 17.

4. It goes without saying that the distinction of moments in the process is for clarity's sake; in practice there is much overlap between the stages. I have been much helped in understanding aspects of this fruitful network of themes by the following works: Simone Deléani, *Christum sequi: Étude d'un thème dans l'oeuvre de saint Cyprien*, Études Augustiniennes, Paris, 1979 and E. J. Tinsley, *The Imitation of God in Christ: An Essay on the Biblical Basis of Christian Spirituality*, SCM Press, London, 1960.

5. Gregory of Nyssa, *On What it Means to Call Oneself a Christian* (FC 54), Virginia Woods Callahan (trans.), Catholic University of America Press, Washington, 1967, p. 85.

6. The words "sympathy" and "compassion" are appropriate here, but they have become debased. Properly both terms signify a fellowship of feeling not limited to suffering. When the Word became incarnate, he consented to share our lot in all things, rejoicing with those that rejoiced and being sad with the sorrowful. Perhaps the strongest indicator of genuine love is when feelings are more linked with the situation of another than with our own.

7. Isaac of Stella, a twelfth-century Cistercian abbot, concludes one of his sermons (8:16) with the following passage: "So, brothers, let Christ be your only master. Let him be for you a book written inside and out (Ephesians 2:14–17). In it read Christ. From it learn Christ. From this original make a

copy of Christ both internally in your hearts and externally in your bodies. The others read in your life the manner of life that Christ lived. This is why it is said (1 Corinthians 6:20), "Glorify and carry God in your bodies." May Christ himself be so kind as to give this gift. Amen." For the text see *SChr* 130, pp. 202–204. An English translation of this sermon was published by Cistercian Publications in 1979.

8. In the expression "grace for grace," the same preposition is used as in the Greek version of the phrase "an eye for an eye and a tooth for a tooth" (Exodus 21:24). It connotes equal measure. To borrow a phrase frequently used by Saint Augustine and subsequent tradition, whatever the Word Incarnate was by nature, we become through grace. God's work in us is the gratuitous gift of divinization: we become "sharers in the divine nature" (2 Peter 1:4).

9. This is not the place to speak at length of the philosophical currents responsible for the switch in focus. In general, from the twelfth to the sixteenth centuries there was a gradual shift of emphasis from being to consciousness. Consequent upon this was an interest in personal or subjective experience that necessarily involved a downgrading of both the objective and the corporate. While the opposite polarities were not officially denied, lack of interest in them meant that in terms of practice they were often overlooked. The more popular the forum, the more considerable the neglect.

10. This has been chronicled ironically and perhaps uncharitably by Ronald Knox in *Enthusiasm: A Chapter in the History of Religion, with Special Reference to the XVII and XVIII Centuries*, Oxford University Press, London, 1950.

11. Conversely, membership of the communion of the Church necessarily involves unity of faith – a common acceptance of revealed truth. This is why baptism is not ordinarily conferred without catechesis, why the Eucharist is restricted to those who profess a common faith, and why all the sacraments are ideally associated with the proclamation of God's word.

12. P. W. Schmiedel in his commentary on Saint John's Gospel listed "a long life" among the requirements for a prospective student of Johannine thought: *Das vierte Evangelium gegenüber den drei ersten*, Tübingen, 1906, p. 61.

13. *De Vitis Patrum, Liber V: Verba Seniorum*, 72; *PL* 73, 966ab.

14. The immediate source of the phrase seems to be the *verbum breviatum* of Romans 9:28, which is a reworking of a quotation of Isaiah 10:22. There may also be a reminiscence of the theme of God's hand not being "abbreviated" as in Isaiah 50:2 and 59:1. Like so many other traditional phrases, the *verbum abbreviatum* theme gains momentum in time. Saint Bernard, for instance,

uses this particular expression sixteen times in the course of his various works.

15. James A. Mohler, S.J., has chosen for the title of his study of Saint Augustine, *A Speechless Child is the Word of God*, New City Press, New York, 1992.

16. Denis also makes an important distinction between two poles evident in discourse about God: *apóphasis* and *katáphasis*. The first recognizes the limits of human language and consequently speaks about God only in negative terms, denying to the divinity any quality that implies inherent limitation. Thus God is named as infinite, beyond space-time, immutable, beyond words and so forth. This style of theology has been especially favored in the Eastern church. *Katáphasis*, on the other hand, has been preferred in the West. It is positive theology, affirming of God whatever is better than its opposite: thus mercy, goodness, fidelity, truth can all be attributed to God in an analogical way. Implicit in such a distinction is the conviction that the divine reality substantially evades human language. The parables of Jesus certainly give us a picture of God – but it is clear from the variety of interpretations that their meaning is not unambiguous. Revelation is given through images and all images are culture-bound, partial, and subject to ambiguity. We cannot look to the Bible for concise definitions, logical deduction, or watertight conclusions. It is a part of the ongoing process of revelation, not its termination.

17. In *Hard Sayings of the Old Testament,* InterVarsity Press, Downers Grove, IL, 1988, Walter C. Kaiser Jr, collects seventy-three obscure or offensive texts of the Old Testament and attempts to explain them simply to the modern reader. While I appreciate the importance of the enterprise, it seems to me that we have to reconcile ourselves to the essential foreignness of the Bible and not feel obliged to defend the worthiness of values that were normal in other times and places. Marketing such texts is extremely difficult because understanding them requires attention not only to their literal meaning but also to their literary techniques and theological presuppositions. Even then, many difficulties remain.

18. Certainly the biblical authors accepted many of the prevailing notions of surrounding cultures – but not all. More often than not we find in the Bible a rejection of the status quo: the Bible is an anthology of narratives and discourses of opposition. Abraham left Ur, Moses left Egypt, Joshua refused to build on already-existing Canaanite cultures, the deuteronomist school was anti-royalist, Amos was anti-prophetic, Jeremiah was anti-priest and Qoheleth anti-Wisdom. Likewise, the New Testament proclaims a vast discontinuity with its immediate environment. Alongside the routine legitimation of the status quo that we find in the Bible there is a strong current of revolutionary thought and prophetic denunciation. That such

anti-establishment diatribes were included in the canon has long been a source both of embarrassment and consolation.

Chapter 3

1. This has been traditionally expressed by the phrase *Amor ipse notitia est*,"Love itself is a form of knowledge." This axiom, taken from Gregory the Great's *Gospel Homilies* (27.4; *PL* 76, 1207a), enjoyed great currency among the spiritual authors of the Middle Ages.

2. There is a fine exposition on this theme by Saint Ephrem the Syrian in his commentary on the Diatessaron (*SChr* 121). "Who is capable of grasping all the richness of even one of your words, O Lord? What we grasp is less than what we leave behind like the thirsty drinking from a single source. The perspectives of your word are as many as the orientations of those who read it" (#52). "What you cannot receive at once because of your weakness, you will receive at another time if you persevere [with reading]" (#53). An English translation of this text is found in *The Roman Breviary* for the Sixth Sunday of the Year.

3. John Cassian, *Conferences* 14.11; *SChr* 54, p. 197.

4. The reason for this assumption is that the present conflated account contains unreconciled traditions of three visitors and one visitor. The Fathers found a "mystery" here. *Tres vidit et unam adoravit*: "He saw three and adored one." It is this interpretation that inspired Rublev's famous icon "The Trinity."

5. The way that the New Testament writers used the Old Testament often demonstrates a certain willingness to be playful with their sources. Matthew's use of Hosea 11:1, "Out of Egypt I have called my son," seems to me a typical example (Matthew 2:15). The author of the first Gospel is mainly concerned to present Jesus' career as the fulfillment of all that God did and promised in the past. He is not attempting to offer a critical exposition of the meaning of the prophetic text. On a subjective level, such easy familiarity with the Scriptures may be more conducive to insight than a cool clinical detachment.

6. This is not the place to discuss the mechanics by which divine inspiration "produced" a written text. There is certainly no question of an inner voice giving verbal dictation. The work of the Spirit is far more interior and allows full scope for the creativity of the writer and for input from others, so that the end result is as much a human product as divine. It is the same principle that operates in the Incarnation. The Bible is, as Christ was, "completely human and completely divine." There are many good treatments of this matter, especially in general commentaries or introductions to the Bible. A landmark essay that defined the question for many and is still of value is John L.

McKenzie, "The Social Character of Inspiration," in *Catholic Biblical Quarterly* 24 (1962), pp. 115–124. This was reprinted in *Myths and Realities: Studies in Biblical Theology*, Geoffrey Chapman, London, 1963, pp. 59–69.

7. Henri de Lubac, *Exégèse médiévale: les quatre sens de l'Écriture*, Aubier (Collection "Théologie"), Paris, four volumes, 1959–1962. An incomplete English translation was published some years ago.

8. The allegorical sense has brought much disrepute to patristic exegesis. Deeply rooted in ancient philosophy, the allegorical method seeks to find a hidden meaning by interpreting the various elements of the text in terms of something entirely different – a little like Freud's dream interpretation. Even in the New Testament we find some examples of the use of "types" (the obvious or visible realities) and "antitypes" (the hidden realities to which the types point). Examples are Galatians 4:24 and Hebrews 8:5. Particularly distressing in those Fathers influenced by Pythagorean thought, was their habit of attributing mystical significance to certain numbers. Thus Augustine explains the 38 years' illness of the man in John 5 thus: 38 = 40–2. That is to say, the cripple represents the Jewish religion; it is perfect (40 is the number of perfection) but it lacks two things: love of God and love of neighbor. Some perfection!

   To us the method seems fanciful and subjective, but there were rules and conventions which offered some safeguards. As poetic improvisations on a theme they are acceptable, if one happens to appreciate such forays. As serious explanations of the literal sense they are hopeless. Saint Bernard of Clairvaux and many of the other monastic authors of the twelfth century considered allegory as something to be used only in the last resort. What is to be praised in the allegorical method is the imaginative will to find in the whole of Scripture a single harmonious revelation. The desire is commendable though the methods used to implement it were inappropriate.

   For a sympathetic survey of the recurrent themes in allegory, see Jean Daniélou, S.J., *From Shadows to Reality: Studies in the Typology of the Fathers*, Burns & Oates, London, 1960. A modern example of the use of allegorical interpretation is Thomas Merton, *Bread in the Wilderness*, New Directions, New York, 1953. Many, including myself, find the book unappealing; those who like it generally do so because they appreciate its poetic qualities. Merton himself, in an evaluation of his writings done on 6 February 1967, classified this work as "less good." For the listing, see Thomas Merton, *Honorable Reader: Reflections on My Work*, Crossroad, New York, 1989, Appendix 2, pp. 150–151. For a positive evaluation of the role of allegory in the evolution of culture see Anna-Teresa Tymieniecka (ed.), *Allegory Revisited: Ideals of Mankind* (Analecta Husserliana xli), Reidel, Dordrecht, 1994.

9. As Saint Augustine says, "Because we are human, we are also weak; because we are weak, we pray". *On the Psalms* 29:2.1; *CChr* 38, p. 174.

10. The word "orthopraxy" (right-doing) was popularized by Edward Schillebeeckx as a complement to "orthodoxy" (right-thinking). See *The Understanding of Faith: Interpretation and Criticism*, Sheed & Ward, London, 1974, pp. 63–70. The use of the term implies that the test of the validity of any interpretation is to be found in the authenticity of its lived response. Theoretical concordance with existing canons is not enough. One could say further that, in some cases, understanding follows performance. We cannot grasp the significance of the radical teaching of the Sermon on the Mount, for instance, unless we attempt to live it. It is in following Jesus' words in practice that the truth of them dawns upon us, and not the other way round.

11. Migne included it in the appendix to Augustine's works under the title *Scala Paradisi*; *PL* 40, 997–1004. A critical text by Edmund Colledge and James Walsh is published in *SChr* 163. An English translation by the same authors has appeared from several publishers: *The Ladder of Monks and Twelve Meditations by Guigo II*, Mowbray, London, 1978; Doubleday (Image Books), Garden City, 1978; and reprinted by Cistercian Publications (CS 48), Kalamazoo, 1981.

12. *RB* 7.

13. *Scala Claustralium* 2; *SChr* 163, pp. 82–84.

14. *Scala Claustralium* 12, *SChr* 163, pp. 106–108. Note that contemplation is said to belong properly to those already in heaven; it is only by privilege, as it were, that it is sometimes tasted in the present life. Thus high spiritual experience was regarded as a foretaste of heaven. This is common teaching among most of the medieval masters. The real summit of the spiritual ascent is heaven.

15. Sermon 38.4; *SChr* 202, p. 292.

16. *Speculum Claustralium* 14; *SChr* 163, p. 112. The interconnection of the stages is mentioned also in the preceding paragraph (13): "These steps are chained together and are so dependent on the service they render one another that the earlier steps are of little or no use without those that follow. Likewise, the later steps rarely eventuate without those that preceded them. What profit is there to occupy time with continual reading and to go over the words and deeds of the saints, unless by chewing over and ruminating on [what we have read] we extract the juice and are able to pass it on to the secret chambers of the heart so that we may consider our own situation and have an enthusiasm to practice the works that we so love to read about. Guigo was aware that the ladder was an image and not the reality itself; to interpret it mechanistically is to rob it of its illustrative force.

17. Quoted by de Lubac, *Exégèse médiévale*, Vol. 2.1, p. 14.

18. *Saint Thérèse of Lisieux: Her Last Conversations* John Clarke, O.C.D. (trans.), I.C.S. Publications, Washington, 1977; The Yellow Notebook, August 4, 1897, No. 5, p. 132.

19. For ordinary queries I use John L. McKenzie, *Dictionary of the Bible*, Geoffrey Chapman, London, 1968. For something more detailed I have recourse to *The Interpreter's Dictionary of the Bible: An Illustrated Encyclopedia*, Abingdon Press, Nashville, 1966 (four volumes). A supplementary fifth volume was published in 1976. More recent are Bruce M. Metzger & Michael D. Coogan (eds.), *The Oxford Companion to the Bible*, Oxford University Press, 1993 (one volume) and David Noel Freedman (ed.), *The Anchor Bible Dictionary*, Doubleday, Garden City, 1992 (six volumes).

20. Thus Gerhard Kittel et al., *Theological Dictionary of the New Testament*, Eerdmans, Grand Rapids, 1964–1984 (ten volumes), and G. Johannes Botterweck et al., *Theological Dictionary of the Old Testament*, Eerdmans, Grand Rapids, 1978 (series incomplete). There is an abridged version of the former available: Geoffrey W. Bromiley, *Theological Dictionary of the New Testament, Abridged in One Volume*, Eerdmans, Grand Rapids, 1985.

21. SCM, London, 1964. A little less accessible is Nigel Turner's *Christian Words*, Thomas Nelson, Nashville, 1981. This is described on the cover thus: "Concise Word Studies to Help Anyone Understand the Unique Vocabulary of the Greek New Testament."

22. Dogmatic Constitution on Divine Revelation, *Dei Verbum*, #12. The same principles have been repeated and expanded since. In November 1993 a long document written by the Pontifical Biblical Commission was published. Entitled "The Interpretation of the Bible in the Church" it was approved by Pope John Paul II and introduced by Cardinal Ratzinger, the Vatican watchdog of orthodoxy. An English translation can be found in *Catholic International* 5.3 (March 1994), pp. 109–147. See also Brendan Byrne, "A New Papal Document on Scripture," *Australasian Catholic Record* 71.3 (July 1994), pp. 325–329. Leslie Houlden remarks, as a compliment, that "most of it could have come from a group of liberal non-Catholic scholars" (*The Times Literary Supplement*, No. 4772 [16 September 1994], p. 15).

23. Such as Bruce M. Metzger, *NRSV Exhaustive Concordance: Includes the Apocryphal and Deuterocanonical Books Complete and Unabridged*, Thomas Nelson, New York, 1991.

24. See, for instance, J. B. Bauer, *Encyclopedia of Biblical Theology: The Complete Sacramentum Verbi*, Crossroad, New York, 1981. Less rigorous is Xavier Léon-Dufour, *Dictionary of Biblical Theology,* HarperSF, 1973.

25. Such as Raymond E. Brown, Joseph A. Fitzmyer & Roland E. Murphy, *The New Jerome Biblical Commentary*, Prentice Hall, Englewood Cliffs, 1990.

26. Raymond E. Brown, *The Gospel According to John* (Anchor Bible 29 and 29A), Doubleday, Garden City, 1966, 1970. Unfortunately, not all the volumes in this series are of the same caliber.

27. Not all popular commentaries are worthwhile; sometimes they do little more than paraphrase the text and throw in a few morsels of information that can easily be gathered from an annotated Bible. A more professional work is sometimes worth the extra effort. A large commentary is not necessarily a good commentary – especially if we are thinking in terms of preparation for *lectio divina*. Here are three examples of excellent thin commentaries that can enhance our biblical reading: James L. Crenshaw, *Ecclesiastes* (Old Testament Library), SCM, London, 1988. Hans Walter Wolff, *Haggai: A Commentary*, Augsburg Publishing House, Minneapolis, 1988; Eduard Lohse, *Colossians and Philemon* (Hermeneia), Fortress Press, Philadelphia, 1971.

28. All the various volumes needed for serious study of the Bible can be obtained on CD-ROM, although these collections are sometimes marked by a fundamentalist bias.

29. *The Complete Parallel Bible: with the Apocryphal/Deuterocanonical Books*, Oxford University Press, 1993. This contains the New Revised Standard Version, the Revised English Bible, the New American Bible and the New Jerusalem Bible.

30. I have written a general survey of this theme in "Mindfulness of God in the Monastic Tradition," *CSQ* 17.2 (1982), pp. 111–126. This is reprinted in M. Casey, *The Undivided Heart: The Western Monastic Approach to Contemplation*, St. Bede's Publications, Petersham, 1994, pp. 62–77.

31. Following these texts through the book of Deuteronomy would be an example of a "walking path" referred to above. Each text that we reflect on broadens our appreciation of the scope of "remembering." As a result, the texts become familiar landmarks in an otherwise strange environment, and we begin to perceive other elements as well.

32. See *Culture and Commitment: A Study of the Generation Gap*, Panther, London, 1972, p. 119.

33. See, for example, Johannes B. Metz, "The Future in the Memory of Suffering," *Concilium* 6.8 (1972), pp. 9–25. Metz writes: "... memory can easily become a 'false consciousness' of our past and an opiate for our present. But there is another form of memory: there are dangerous memories, memories which make demands on us ... They break through the canon of all that is taken as self-evident and unmask as deception the certainty of those 'whose hour is always here' (Jn. 7.6). They seem to subvert

our structures of plausibility. Such memories are like dangerous and incalculable visitants from the past. They are memories we have to take into account; memories, as it were, with a future content" (pp. 14–15).

34. Aelred of Rievaulx compared the act of memory to a loving embrace which brings us to communion with God. "Memory is like the soul's embrace by which it clings to God without any forgetfulness" (sermon *in natitivate Domini* in C. H. Talbot [ed.], *Sermones Inediti B. Aelredi Abbatis Rievallensis*, Editiones Cistercienses, Rome, 1952, p. 38). "So the human being embraces his God through memory without any sense of fatigue" (sermon *in die Pentecosten*, id., p. 108.) On the other hand, William of St. Thierry saw memory not as an act but as a faculty; for him memory was the bedroom in which the union occurred (*In cant* 76; *SChr* 82, p. 186).

35. This is the point made by Alexander Solzhenitsyn in the address which followed his reception of the 1983 Templeton Prize for Religion. "And if I were called upon to identify briefly the principal trait of the *entire* twentieth century, here too, I would be unable to find anything more precise and pithy than to repeat once again: 'Men have forgotten God.' The failings of human consciousness deprived of its divine dimension, have been a determining factor in all the major crimes of this century." *The Orthodox Monitor* 15 (January to July 1983), p. 3.

36. Thus Bernard of Clairvaux writes (*sent.* 1.12; *SBO* 6b.10.18–22): "The memory of God is the pathway to the presence of God. Those who keep the commandments in mind with a view to observing them will be rewarded, from time to time, by perceiving the presence of God."

37. SC 11.12; *SBO* 1.55.12–19.

38. *Conference* 1.22; *SChr* 42, p. 107.

Chapter 4

1. Businesses that allow employees to work at home via computer link usually insist that the work is done in a businesslike environment and not at a kitchen table while minding children. Some prescribe an office separate from the living quarters and even the wearing of appropriate attire. Clearly in such institutions ambience is regarded as contributing significantly to the quality of the work done. Maybe the children of this world are wiser in their generation than the children of light!

2. Here I am talking about individuals reading on their own. Later I will discuss reading with others. A secure environment is perhaps even more important when more than one are involved.

3. Someone remarked to me recently that she remembers in greater detail the

books she reads in large-print format. This assertion seems credible to me, though I know of no experimental data that supports it.

4. There are many suitable prayers in the collection *Proclaiming All Your Wonders: Prayers for a Pilgrim People*, Vincent Ryan and Nivard Kinsella (trans.), Liturgical Press, Collegeville, MN, 1992. These prayers were written for use in the Liturgy of the Hours, but are also excellent for private and occasional use.

5. See Jerome Kodell, O.S.B., "*Lectio Divina* and the Prayer Journal," *Review for Religious* 39 (1980), pp. 582–591.

6. Medieval monastic regulations provided that monks did not bury their heads in their hoods while reading – the implication being that the warm, dark, and private space thus created made it easy for them to nod off.

7. See my article "From the Silence of God to the God of Silence: The Experience of Progress in *Lectio Divina*," *Tjurunga* 43 (1993), pp. 3–24.

8. See Romans 7:23. Although Saint Paul is probably referring to the plight of the unbaptized, centuries of subsequent commentators have seen in the lament of this chapter the Christian experience of being not yet fully redeemed and consequently still somewhat in bondage to the power of sin.

9. See Aldous Huxley, *The Devils of Loudun*, Penguin Books, Harmondsworth, 1971, pp. 188–189.

10. In *The Australian Hymn Book*, Dove, Melbourne, 1992, this is No. 488.

11. This was my concern in "Seven Principles of *Lectio Divina*," *Tjurunga* 12 (1976), pp. 69–74; reprinted in *The Undivided Heart*, pp. 4–9.

12. Sometimes it is only possible to maintain the fiction of our blamelessness by downsizing our prayer-related activities. If we avoid the situations where formerly we encountered God, then God's silence is not so vociferous. Genuine *lectio divina* is left aside in favor of study and informational reading. Or it is omitted altogether.

13. *On Penitence*, *PG* 49, 282d.

14. John Cassian speaks well of this experience: "The mind is shaped during its prayer [and also in *lectio divina*] by what it was beforehand. When we prostrate ourselves in prayer, our previous actions, words, and impressions continue to play before the minds of our imagination, just as they did before, making us angry or sad, or causing us to relive past lusts or foolish laughter. I am ashamed to admit that we are even entertained by comic words and deeds and our mind is diverted by recalling conversations we have had previously" (*Conference* 9.3; *SChr* 54, p. 42).

15. Aelred of Rievaulx, *Sermo in Adventu Domini*, # 11; *PL* 184, 823ab.

Chapter 5

1. It is to be noted with regret that almost all "patristic" writers are "Fathers" and not "Mothers." If I continue the ordinary usage of "patrology," "patristic," and "Church Fathers" it is simply a recognition of statistical reality and not a sign of approval. Where the evidence warrants it, I try to find inclusive terms. In general, patristic authors are the great bishops, preachers, and teachers of the first millennium. They are usually classified first according to the language in which they wrote – Greek, Latin, or Syriac, for instance – then by region or school of thought: African, Alexandrian, Cappadocian, and so forth.

2. I am always wary of "drill-sergeant theology," that marshals all the Fathers into orderly array and attempts to parade them as a single cohesive group. There are few points that meet the criterion of Vincent of Lérins ("what has been believed everywhere, always and by all"): mostly the Fathers exhibit only a precarious unanimity. Collectively they serve better as sources of insight and depth than as propagators of a single party line.

3. *RB* 73:3–4.

4. Individual entries in the recently finished *Dictionnaire de Spiritualité* often succeed in accomplishing this; perhaps some day we will have something comparable in English.

5. *Tjurunga* 12 (1976), pp. 75–83. In the same issue there is an article by Vincent Desprez, "How Readable are the Fathers Today?", pp. 85–93.

6. See the later section of this chapter, "An Impressionistic Survey of the Literature," pp. 126–130.

7. *Patres Ecclesiae* of January 2, 1980. An official English translation appears in *Osservatore Romano [Weekly Edition]* 8 (621) of 25 February 1980, pp. 6–9.

8. *The Pope Speaks* 35.3 (May/June 1990), pp. 167–187.

9. See also Thomas Spidlik (ed.), *Drinking from the Hidden Fountain: A Patristic Breviary: Ancient Wisdom for Today's World*, Cistercian Publications, Kalamazoo, 1994.

10. The difficulty of feeling at home with the (translated) language of the Fathers is particularly acute in those young churches where English may be a second (or third) language. A.I.M., a monastic agency responsible for implanting monasticism in different cultures, has, since 1990, produced a series of small patristic works in Basic English. They are like the condensed books brought out by *Reader's Digest*: simple syntax and vocabulary and abridgment of complicated matter, but aiming to convey both the content and the feeling of the original. The series is entitled "Witnesses for Christ" and includes the Didache, the letters of Ignatius of Antioch, Tertullian on Prayer, and Bernard on the Love of God. Copies are available from Stanbrook Abbey, Worcester, England.

11. The classic example of this genre is Peter Brown, *Augustine of Hippo: A Biography*, Faber & Faber, London, 1967. Not all biographies achieve his brilliant combination of scholarly clarity and accessibility to the general reader. A two-volume biography of Chrysostom that I enjoyed was Chrysostomos Baur, *John Chrysostom and his Time*, Sands, London, 1959 & 1960.

12. What was written in letters, as distinct from the oral message given to the bearer, was usually of a semi-public nature. The letters have been preserved because they are often mini-treatises on particular topics or examples of how to deal with particular situations. Among those whose correspondence is available in English are: Ambrose, Athanasius, Augustine, Basil, Cyprian, Gregory Nazianzen, Jerome, John Chrysostom, Leo.

13. See my article "Western (Latin) Spirituality" in Downey (ed.), *The New Dictionary of Catholic Spirituality*, pp. 1021–1027.

14. This is the title of a famous book by the great expert on Western monasticism, Jean Leclercq; the second edition was published by SPCK, London, in 1978.

15. Public reading in the monasteries included the patristic readings in the liturgy, as provided in the Rule of Saint Benedict, reading at meals, and a period of communal reading at the end of the day, the "collation."

16. The contents of medieval libraries is not a matter of guesswork. It is the object of much intensive study. For example, Anne Bondéelle-Souchier, *Bibliothèques cisterciennes dans la France médiévale: Répertoire des abbayes d'hommes*, CNRS, Paris, 1991. We know what books were available at particular periods.

17. For those interested in documenting this assertion, I have given a listing of overlapping studies that develop aspects of twelfth century life in "Bernard of Clairvaux: Forty Years of Scholarship" in John S. Martin (ed.), *St. Bernard of Clairvaux: The Man*, University of Melbourne, 1991, footnote 43, pp. 40–41.

18. *Ultimus inter Patres sed primis certe non impar.* This is to be found in the *Praefatio generalis* to the many reprints of his edition of Bernard's *Opera omnia*, #23.

19. See my "Thomas Merton within a Tradition of Prayer," *CSQ* 13 (1979), pp. 372–378; *CSQ* 14 (1980), pp. 81–92. Reprinted in Patrick Hart (ed.), *The Legacy of Thomas Merton* (CS 92), Cistercian Publications, Kalamazoo, 1986, pp. 25–47.

20. In what follows I am indebted to the famous article of René Arnou, "Platonisme des Pères," in the *Dictionnaire de théologie Catholique*, 12, cols. 2258–2392. The article first appeared in 1935 and many of its generalizations

would be questioned today, but as a survey of the issues involved in this question it is unsurpassed. See also Endre von Ivánka, *Plato Christianus: La réception critique du platonisme chez les Pères de l'Église*, Presses Universitaires de France, Paris, 1990; A. H. Armstrong (ed.), *The Cambridge History of Later Greek and Early Medieval Philosophy*, Cambridge University Press, 1970, especially pp. 425–533; Pierre-Thomas Camelot, "Hellenisme," *DSp* 7, cols 145–164; Marcia M. Colish, *The Stoic Tradition from Antiquity to the Early Middle Ages*, Brill, Leiden, 1985.

21. When he spoke against the inclusion of Aristotelianism in theology, Martin Luther was defending the older platonizing tradition of the Fathers. His conclusion was that "the whole Aristotle is to theology as darkness is to light." See his "Disputation against Scholastic Theology" in Timothy F. Lull, *Martin Luther's Basic Theological Writings*, Augsburg Fortress, Minneapolis, 1989, p. 16.

22. For a study of how this theme built up to a climax in the twelfth century, see Robert Javelet, *Image et ressemblance au douzième siècle: De saint Anselme à Alain de Lille*, Éditions Letouzey & Ané, Paris, 1967. See also Stephan Otto, *Die Funktion des Bildesbegriffes in der Theologie des 12. Jahrhunderts*, Aschendorff, Münster, 1963.

23. See Aimé Solignac, "Mémoire," *DSp* 10, cols 991–1002; Hermann Josef Sieben, "Mnèmè Theou," *DSp* 10, cols 1407–1414.

24. It is commonly attributed to Bernard of Clairvaux, but this is incorrect. It was probably composed in England toward the end of the twelfth century, certainly under the influence of Bernard. See André Wilmart, *Le "Jubilus" dit de saint Bernard: Étude avec textes*, Edizioni di storia e letteratura, Rome, 1944. The hymn appears as no. 126 in *The Australian Hymn Book*.

25. See my article, "Apatheia" in Downey (ed.), *The New Dictionary of Catholic Spirituality*, pp. 50–51.

26. This is contrary to the well-circulated views of such authors as Dodds and Festugière that the ascetic movement derived from a contempt of the human condition due to "Platonic dualism." The ancient monks had a clear awareness of the shared momentum of body and soul, and they knew by experience that the battle for the heart was fought on the psychosomatic frontier. "Seldom, in ancient thought, had the body been seen as more deeply implicated in the transformation of the soul" (Peter Brown, *The Body and Society: Men, Women and Sexual Renunciation in Early Christianity,* Faber, London, 1989, p. 235).

27. The notion of participation became quite important in the thinking of Thomas Aquinas. See L-B. Geiger, *La participation dans la philosophie de S. Thomas d'Aquin.* Vrin, Paris, 1953.

28. I have given a coverage of this theme in *Athirst for God: Spiritual Desire in Bernard of Clairvaux's Sermons on the Song of Songs* (CS 77), Cistercian Publications, Kalamazoo, 1988.

29. Plotinus, *Sixth Ennead*, 11; translated by Stephen McKenna and B. S. Page in *The Great Books of the Western World*, 17, Encyclopaedia Britannica, Chicago, 1952, p. 360.

30. There is a giant article on contemplation by an extremely competent group of writers in *DSp* 2, cols. 1643–2193. There is a treatment of the theme in Plato, Plotinus and others by René Arnou in columns 1716–1742. The interreligious aspects of contemplative experience are explored in Moshe Idel and Bernard McGinn (eds), *Mystical Union and Monotheistic Faith: An Ecumenical Dialogue*, Macmillan, New York, 1989.

31. *Republic*, Book 6, 490; *Timaeus*, 90.

32. See the articles under the heading, "Divinisation" in *DSp* 3, cols 1370–1459.

33. A thirty-eight volume re-edition of *ANF* and both series of *NPNF* with a new annotated index has appeared from Hendrickson Publishers; it is considerably more expensive than the Eerdmans reprint; the advertised price is US$1,100.

34. For example, John Cassian's *Conference* 22 is omitted in its entirety. See Series Two, Vol. 11, p. 519.